RICH POOR PEOPLE

Kwaku Agyeman

Unless otherwise indicated, all Scripture quotations in this volume are from the New King James Version of the Bible.

Rich Poor People

© 2019 Kwaku Agyeman

All rights reserved under international copyright law. Written permission must be secured from the publisher to use or reproduce any part of this book. No part of this book may be reproduced in any form or by any means without prior written permission from the author, except for brief quotations in critical reviews or articles.

Table of Contents

1. If Christ Cannot Be Poor You Cannot Be Poor 1
2. Seek First The Kingdom 7
3. Don't Set Your Heart On Material Things 11
4. Redeemed From The Curse Of Poverty 13
5. Prosperity Is Not Materialism 16
6. Poverty Is Not A Blessing 21
7. Poverty Is Not A Rite Of Passage 24
8. Financial Insufficiency Is A Choice 32
9. Slaves of Prosperity 36
10. The Covenant Blessing Of Abraham 40
11. You Have Power To Get Wealth 45
12. God Teaches You To Profit 48
13. Made Rich In Christ 53
14. Your Prosperity Is In Your Mandate 58
15. Ambassadors of Christ 62
16. Blessed With Every Spiritual Blessing 69
17. You Are Master Of Your Destiny 74
18. The Key To Prosperity 84
19. Your Wealth Is A Spiritual Reality 91
20. Bridging The Manifestation Gap 98
21. The Truth Set Me Free 103
22. About The Author 106
23. Acknowledgements 107

Preface

Financial insufficiency has become one of the devil's favourite weapons in his fight against the Body of Christ. Consequently a significant number of Christians are facing extreme financial challenges, though they are rich in reality. They live in the world as 'rich poor people'- people who are rich yet paradoxically live in penury. Rich poor people struggle financially for the most part because they are oblivious of their wealth in Christ Jesus.

In this book I provide divinely inspired biblical truths aimed at helping bring people' out of the darkness of poverty into the light of God's prosperity.

This is achieved by deprogramming the minds of people caught up in the web of poverty through inaccurate 'worldly' and Christian teachings. This book helps rid their minds of the myths and sacred traditions that have helped impoverish them.

I then seek to help renew their minds with the timeless truths of the Gospel of Christ to set them free from the bondage of poverty. This is necessary because to come out of the bondage of poverty, your mind must first be made rich.

Therefore, in this book you will discover the truth of your divine wealth in Christ Jesus. You will also learn how to assume the position of who and what the Word of God says you are in Christ. Amen.

Chapter One

If Christ Cannot Be Poor You Cannot Be Poor

In order for you to become poor Christ must first become poor. If Christ cannot be poor, you cannot be poor. This statement may cause you to blink, but it is true. This is a timeless truth that should be embossed in your mind for the duration of your natural life on earth. The day you accepted Christ as your Saviour you became one with Him and He took over your life. The 'poor, powerless you' ceased to exist and a new Christ empowered person took the place of your former self.

Galatians 2:20

I have been crucified with Christ

It is no longer I who live, but Christ lives in me

And the life which I now live in the flesh

I live by faith in the Son of God Who loved me and gave His life for me

For many years I failed to realize the source of my wealth and prosperity was founded in Christ. I lived under the impression that prosperity was tied only to a business idea and hard work. I spent much of the time searching for that business idea that would represent my breakthrough but without much success. I tried to establish a number of potentially lucrative business concepts, however, none of them amounted to anything. My business ventures appeared to start well, but ended badly. I had opportunities but they never bore fruit.

Something was definitely wrong, but what was it? It took me some time to realize what I had been doing wrong. My mistake was in appointing myself as the 'enabler' of my well-being. In other words I took over from God as the source of my blessing and made 'my business' my business.

If Christ is the Lord of your life, your business CANNOT be your business. Your business is God's business because you have become one with Him.

By making my business my business, I had taken on the responsibility of ensuring my financial well-being and success. I had erroneously assumed responsibility for my own increase, which you can't do as a child of God. By which power do you hope to have your increase manifest? It is God who 'manifests' increase. It has absolutely nothing to do with you.

To experience increase in your life, your mind must first be made rich in Christ. Your mind must be renewed to accept Christ as the source of your wealth and not what you do to earn income. This knowledge is crucial in experiencing the manifestation of your divine wealth. It is the turning point. If you get to understand this, you will never be poor in your life.

Your financial prosperity is not in what you do, but in what Christ has done. You are rich by default because Christ with whom you have become one is rich. Therefore you are prosperous because Christ is prosperous and you contribute nothing to make that happen.

The truth is that you are rich even before you engage in any income generating enterprise. You may be unemployed but that does nothing to affect your wealthy status. The enterprise you are engaged in technically contributes nothing to make you rich. The success of your enterprise is only the manifestation of your wealth in Christ.

Your wealth is divinely ordained and only seeks a channel through which it can be released. Thus if you are idle, remain idle no longer. Idleness will prevent the manifestation of your wealth. Your wealth is impatiently waiting to be birthed. Wealth requires an avenue to 'show forth'; it can't be expressed in a vacuum. Without gainful employment or enterprise your wealth CANNOT and will not materialize.

Just as water is fetched for use with a 'container', wealth must be 'fetched' with work. So your hand must find something to do. Prayer and fasting without work won't get it done. Find something to do and quickly. It doesn't matter what kind of honest employment or business, you engage yourself in. You are guaranteed to prosper in it. It doesn't depend on your self-effort. It's about the effort of Christ and what He's attained on your behalf.

You can declare with certainty that you will never be broke or poor. And this claim is true because Christ cannot be broke or poor. That is the real meaning of being like Christ. It's a complete union with Christ. His life has become one with yours and so has His finances. Your life and finances no longer exist separate from His life and finances.

The universal church to which all believers belong also represents the Body of Christ. Jesus is the head of the Body and we are members of the Body. Therefore if you are the Body of Christ, with Christ as the head of the Body, you are one entity with Christ. Up to this point many of you have seen Jesus as a person separate from you. But He is not and can't be. You are one inseparable unit with Christ. As the head and body of Christ constitutes one entity, they are affected equally by anything that affects the 'entity', such as wealth or sickness.

1 Corinthians 12:27

Now you are the body of Christ and members individually.

Colossians 1:18

And He is the head of the body the church…

Therefore the Head can't be rich without the body. Meaning Christ can't be rich without His Body. So if Christ can't be poor His body can't be poor. Since you are the Body of Christ, you can't be poor. Whatever attributes Christ possesses you possess also.

You could also say the body can't be poor without the Head. Therefore, if the body is poor, the Head must also be poor. But since the Head (Christ) CANNOT be poor, the body CANNOT be poor. This is why you can never be poor in your lifetime, because for you to be poor, Christ must first become poor. Even the devil knows he can't make you poor. The devil is only able to steal your wealth through your ignorance of who you are in Christ.

Don't base prosperity on what you do or how you do it. Neither should you bank your hopes on a government, or the economy of a nation. Under no circumstances should you rely on a man irrespective of their capabilities or resourcefulness.

Jesus could only take your place of sin and give you His life of righteousness by becoming spiritually one with you. When you became one with Christ, you receive of His fullness. In other words, every grace Christ is filled with can be found in you. Everything accessible in Christ is available in you.

John 1:16

And of His fullness we have all received

And grace for grace

You have received every grace that is in Christ. You have received the wisdom, knowledge, mercy, faith, wealth, love, joy, compassion, strength, divine health, peace, fruitfulness and eternal life of Christ Jesus.

You Are Inextricably Linked With The Riches of Christ

You're inextricably linked with the riches of Christ because you're inextricably linked with Him. The reason why poverty shouldn't be able to claim you is because the spirit of poverty can't separate you from Christ and become one with you. You are not blessed and rich as a child of God just because you are good or generous. You are blessed and rich because of your spiritual union with Christ.

1 Corinthians 6:17

But he who is joined to the Lord is one spirit with Him

Ephesians 5:29-32

For no one ever hated his own flesh, but nourishes and cherishes it

Just as the Lord does the church.

For we are members of His body, of His flesh and of His bones.

For this reason a man shall leave his father and mother

And be joined to his wife

And the two shall become one flesh.

This is a great mystery but I speak concerning Christ and the church.

Please understand that your union with Christ is not figurative. You have literally become one spirit and body with Christ Jesus. In the same sense your financial standing has become a reflection of the financial standing of Christ. Just as a husband and wife become joined in marriage as one flesh, your finances and that of Christ Jesus have become one.

All Christ has is yours. Hallelujah!! It's not possible for you ever to be poor. Be reassured that no demon in hell can engineer your financial separation from Christ. What God has put together no demon can put asunder.

Heir of God Through Christ

Christ has made you an heir of the Most High God - Creator and owner of all wealth. As long as you remain in Christ, you remain an heir of God, which leaves you rich for the duration of your time on earth. You can't be poor because you have access to the inestimable wealth of God. As an n heir of God you can't be a slave to poverty.

Galatians 4:7

Therefore you are no longer a slave,

But a son and if a son

Then an heir of God through Christ.

Jesus was poor in spirit (humble) during His time on earth but not poor financially. He took on the form of a servant and made Himself of no reputation in order to get you out of poverty.

2 Corinthians 8:9

For you know the grace of our Lord Jesus Christ

That though He was rich yet for your sakes He became poor

That you through His poverty might become rich

Jesus was not made an heir to poverty. Poverty has no place in Christ Jesus and it can't have any place in you. Jesus is rich and so are you.

Chapter Two
Seek First The Kingdom

Mathew 6:31-33

Therefore do not worry saying 'what shall we eat?'

Or 'what shall we drink?' or what shall we wear?'

For after all these things the Gentiles seek.

For your heavenly Father knows that you need all these things.

But seek first the Kingdom of God and His righteousness

And all these things shall be added to you'

For many years as a Christian, I didn't particularly appreciate and understand the verses of scripture in 'Mathew 6:31-33'. However, when I received revelation concerning these verses, it strengthened my belief concerning my wealth in Christ.

They helped confirm and establish for me that Christ indeed was the source of prosperity. I realized it was a waste of time seeking prosperity on my own. You won't find true prosperity without Christ. You may find something resembling prosperity without Him, but I don't think it's the kind you want. Prosperity without Christ is not fulfilling and comes with a lot of baggage.

Prosperity that is all-inclusive and fulfilling is available only in the Kingdom of God. The Kingdom of God exists with Christ at its center. To seek the Kingdom of God requires that you focus on Christ Jesus. The access rights to the Kingdom of God are vested in Christ Jesus that is why you must work on building your relationship with Him.

The Key To Kingdom Benefits

Many Christians, though rich in reality, endure a life of hardship and financial insufficiency. This state of affairs exists because they fail to appropriate and experience the benefits of belonging to the Kingdom of God. The moment you acknowledge Christ as your Saviour, you automatically become a citizen of the Kingdom of Heaven and a beneficiary of the Kingdom of God.

The Kingdom of Heaven is the location where God and His heavenly hosts dwell. But the Kingdom of God is a system of divine influence over which God superintends through Christ. The Kingdom of Heaven is a location but the Kingdom of God is a spiritual experience. You should know this difference so you can engage the way you're supposed to. The Kingdom of Heaven and the Kingdom of God refer to different things.

Luke 17:20-21

Now when He was asked by the Pharisees when the Kingdom of God would come

He answered them and said,

The Kingdom of God does not come with observation;

Nor will they say, See here! Or 'See there'!

For indeed, the Kingdom of God is within you

The Kingdom of God is the embodiment of the 'new world order' that came into existence with the emergence of Christ Jesus. It's the governance system of God by which the new creation in Christ Jesus is supposed to live. It's a supernatural existence lived in the knowledge that man is a spirit being governed by spiritual realities. Spiritual realities refer to the eternal truths in the Word established by Christ as an inheritance for the saints of God. One such spiritual reality is your divine wealth in Christ.

The Kingdom of God is ultimately a 'Christ centered' living experience. It's a spiritual environment that enables the new man in Christ appropriate the inheritance made available by God for His children.

To 'seek first the kingdom of God' – is to subject yourself to His Word and will. The life you led in the past without Christ must come to an end. Now you must live, move and establish your existence in Christ. It's after this that all other things including divine wealth becomes available to you. This is the key to enjoying the rights established and available to you in the Kingdom of God.

The ultimate mystery of Christianity is revealed in the truth that God has put everything you will ever need from Him in Christ. The source of everything God has given to mankind is Jesus Christ. Every blessing from God is available ONLY in Christ Jesus. From atonement to redemption, salvation, peace, joy, rest, fruitfulness, strength, wisdom, wealth and longevity - they are all available in Christ Jesus. No one but Christ can provide it.

These blessings constitute what one can find in the Kingdom of God. Because all the blessings in the Kingdom are vested in Christ, you must embrace Christ to gain access to them. You can't obtain what God provides without first seeking Christ Jesus. 'Seek ye first the Kingdom of God'- simply means acknowledging and embracing the lordship of Christ Jesus over your life.

When you become a citizen of the Kingdom of Heaven, you automatically gain access to the wealth and prosperity of God. You don't even have to pray for it. It is yours by default. You don't need to pray to be made rich, because you are already rich. The system through which you appropriate these blessings is the Kingdom of God; which is within you (Luke 17:21) because Christ is in you.

Colossians 1:27

To them God willed to made known

What are the riches of the glory of the mystery among the Gentiles

Which is Christ in you, the hope of glory

Every need you have can be met through the Kingdom of God. Therefore there is no need pursuing men for favours and opportunities. Stop chasing after the 'false' prosperity offered by men. Rather spend time chasing after the Kingdom of God.

How do you seek the Kingdom of God? You do so by seeking Jesus. First acknowledge Him as your Lord and Saviour. Then continue to seek Him through fellowship and diligent study of the Word of God. The more you study and know the truth, the more tangible the Kingdom of God and its blessings will become to you. You must also have a desire to know Christ and what it means to be in spiritual union with Him.

When you gain understanding of your spiritual union with Christ, you would have attained the ultimate goal of seeking the Kingdom of God. Once this happens, all things, including wealth that are already yours, shall become evident. You won't need to pray for anything because God knows you have need of them and has provided them to you through Christ.

Your Wealth Is Not In Material Possessions

When you seek the Kingdom of God, you will come to understand that wealth is not measured by material possessions. The wealth of a Christian is vested in Christ and not in his or her visible material gain.

Your money and material possessions only help provide an indication of your financial standing. But they don't give a true measure of the totality of your wealth. The true measure of your wealth is inestimable because it is linked to the inestimable wealth of Christ.

Don't cry or worry over your apparent lack of material possessions. You are rich, even though you may have nothing physical or material to show. Your mind must first be awakened to the reality of your wealth before its manifestation can take place. When you retire to bed thank God for your wealth in Christ and wake up in the morning thanking Him. Be excited by it and embrace it forcefully.

Never say, 'I don't have money'. You have money in abundance; more money than you could ever need. Everything that belongs to God belongs to Christ and everything that Christ owns is yours. The wealth of God is the wealth of Christ and the wealth of Christ is your wealth. You have more money in Christ than you'll ever need in your life.

Don't Set Your Heart On Material Things

Don't set your heart on material things because they don't constitute your wealth. If you happen to lose any material possessions, you lose nothing. They are merely possessions and can easily be replaced. You have not lost anything because you have not lost Christ. If you remain inextricably linked to Christ, then every material possession is still available to you.

Even if you lose physical possessions, the source of all possessions remains in you. Scripture gives an account of a rich man who had an encounter with Jesus in his quest for eternal life. However, when Jesus asked the rich man to sell all his possessions and come follow Him, the rich man couldn't comply and went away sad.

Mathew 19:16-22

Now behold, one came and said to Him, 'Good Teacher, what good thing shall I do that I may have eternal life? So He said to him, 'Why do you call me good? No one is good but One, that is God. But if you want to enter into life, keep the commandments'. He said to Him, "which ones"? Jesus said, "you shall not murder, you shall not commit adultery, you shall not steal, you shall not bear false witness. Honour your father and your mother, and, you shall love your neighbour as yourself". The young man said to Him, "All these things I have kept from my youth. "What do I still lack"? Jesus said to him, "If you want to be perfect, go sell what you have and give to the poor, and you will have treasure in heaven; and come follow Me".

The rich young ruler went away saddened because he thought his possessions represented his wealth. Therefore, to lose his material possessions, for him meant the total loss of his wealth. Consequently he failed to comply with what Jesus asked him to do.

He failed to recognize his wealth was in Christ and not in the material possessions he was anxious to hold onto. When your wealth is in Christ, whatever material things you give away or lose can always be gotten back. It can't be lost because the source of the material possessions can't be lost.

If the rich young ruler had accepted to follow Christ, he would have linked himself to an everlasting source of wealth that never dries up. Christ is the embodiment of the Kingdom of God. If you seek Him first, wealth and everything else shall be added to you.

When you have Christ in your life you can boldly claim; 'I will never be poor in my life'. It is not a boast in your material wealth. It is a boast in Christ and in His inestimable wealth. Because your wealth is in Christ you should not be afraid to give away any material possession. Material possessions are merely manifestations of your wealth and not the totality of your wealth.

Chapter Three

Redeemed From The Curse Of Poverty

For many people when they take a retrospective look at their lives, all they can see is failure, poverty and misery. They find themselves caught up in a vicious cycle of financial insufficiency with no end in sight.

Jesus Has Set You Free

But if you are a believer, you ought to know Jesus has liberated you from the scourge of financial insufficiency. You have been delivered from the curse of poverty. You have also been redeemed from any generational curse that may have plagued members of your family for as long as you can remember. You have been redeemed by the Blood of Jesus from anything that contrives to keep you poor.

Perhaps your adverse financial situation could be the result of an ancestral transgression, you have no knowledge of. It could even be the consequence of your own infractions. But whatever the nature or cause of your situation, Jesus has redeemed you from it. All it takes to enjoy your financial redemption is to believe and receive what Jesus has done by faith. Financial redemption is as much a fruit of salvation as the forgiveness of sins.

The Curse Of The Law

What is the curse of the law? It represents the punishment and consequences that came upon a person for disobeying the commandments of God under the Old Covenant. The first five books of the Old Testament provide a comprehensive picture of what constitutes the law and the curse of the law respectively.

Until the coming of Christ and the righteousness He made available, the Law was the life manual for man. It was the standard by which man endeavoured to attain right sanding in the sight of God. Failure to meet the tenets of the law resulted in the unleashing of the wrath of God.

The expression of God's wrath on a breacher of the law took the form of a curse, which came to be known as the Curse of the Law. The consequences resulting from the breach of the law were threefold - namely sickness, poverty and spiritual death. However, after Jesus atoned for the sins of mankind the Curse of Law was effectively repealed.

Galatians 3:13

Christ has redeemed us from the curse of the law

Having become a curse for us

(For it is written, 'Cursed is everyone who hangs on a tree')

After the death of Jesus, man was restored to good standing with God and poverty as a curse over man was removed forever. Man was liberated from this curse by the payment of a ransom in the form of the precious blood of Jesus.

Jesus reversed the curses resulting from the sinful nature passed down by Adam and replaced them with blessings and the nature of righteousness, obtainable by those who accept Christ as Lord and Saviour. So in the place of sickness He made available divine health. Instead of poverty He provided prosperity and for spiritual death He gave eternal life. Hallelujah!

You Are Guaranteed Financial Freedom

Your redemption from the curse of poverty through Christ Jesus guarantees you lifelong financial freedom. Once redeemed by the blood of Jesus, poverty has no legal or moral right to lay its cold icy hands on you. Redemption is synonymous with financial independence. You have no business living on 'Barely Getting Along Street' any longer. The new address to which you've been moved is ' Blessed Beyond Measure Street'.

Poverty's dominion over you has been broken. Every circumstance that allowed poverty to claim you as a victim has been taken care of. All your debts, both spiritual and financial have been cancelled. Any financial debt you owe has been taken care of by your redemption through Christ Jesus. You must literally believe this and experience the physical manifestation in your life.

Your redemption is total and all encompassing. Not only have your indebtedness in respect of sin been paid off; every other debt you owed has also been taken care of. Christ Jesus has attained excellent 'credit ratings' in both spiritual and financial terms for you.

Don't believe only in the cancellation of your sins. You must also believe in the deliverance from financial liabilities and indebtedness. Jesus paid the price with His life to save man from bondage in all forms and manifestation. Financial lack represents a form of bondage and anyone experiencing a state of financial lack is under bondage. But Jesus came into the world to set free, all those under all forms of bondage including financial bondage.

Romans 5:8-9

But God demonstrates His own love toward us
In that while we were still sinners Christ died for us
Much more then having now been justified by His blood
We shall be saved from wrath through Him

The blood of Jesus has justified you. Every form of indebtedness in your life has been taken care of. Your God is able to supply all your needs according to His riches in Christ Jesus. Therefore develop the mindset that financial burdens have no place in your life. You have been saved from the wrath (displeasure of God) that facilitated the entrance of poverty into the life of man.

The grounds for your association with poverty no longer exist. Jesus has taken care of the cause for the curse. Therefore the curse of poverty has no basis to afflict you let alone prevail over you.

Chapter Four
Prosperity Is Not Materialism

Prosperity is not materialism. Nonetheless many in the Body of Christ have taken the flawed position of linking prosperity with materialism. This has unwittingly led some Christians down the path of financial hardship as they shun wealth to avoid being tagged as materialistic.

Materialism is the unbridled desire and quest for riches and material possessions. It has nothing to do with wealth or prosperity. Prosperity may manifest in the possession of material things. But the possession of material things does not make one materialistic. However some 'anti- rich' Christians have linked materialism with prosperity and live in fear the acquisition of wealth can possibly send them to hell.

Consequently they have no desire for wealth and are quick to tag anybody who is rich as materialistic. In their opinion it's wrong for a man of God to live in a mansion. They question why a minister of the gospel should own a plane or have more than one car. Did Jesus not say blessed are those who are poor in spirit'? - They ask.

This is a question you may or may not have heard before. But it's a position often espoused by people who believe in the doctrine of 'poverty is next to godliness'. It may sound outlandish; but sadly this doctrine is still preached and practiced.

Jesus did not say, 'blessed are those who are poor financially'. He said, 'blessed are the poor in spirit' (Mathew 5:3). 'Poor in spirit' connotes humility and brokenness. People who are poor in spirit are those who have yielded themselves to Christ. They depend entirely on God and not on any attribute of theirs. They recognize their sufficiency is in Christ and not of themselves.

The poor in spirit are meek and humble before God. Meekness and humility are attributes of people who acknowledge the need for a Saviour. In essence the statement Jesus made about people who were 'poor in spirit' had nothing to do with finances. Nor did it refer to the financial status of those He was preaching to.

Anti-rich Christians have also misinterpreted the encounter between Jesus and the rich young ruler (Mathew 19:16-22) in the Bible to buttress their doctrine'. In their view, it 'proves' it's next to impossible for rich people to get to heaven. This, unfortunately, is a blatant untruth manufactured from the 'falsehood factory' located in hell.

Abraham was undoubtedly one of the richest if not the richest man in his time. Can anybody make the claim that Abraham failed to make it to heaven because he was rich? Abraham is in heaven (Luke 16:22-31). How about Job and Joseph respectively? Job was the richest man in the part of the world where he lived. Joseph was the Prime Minister of the richest nation during his lifetime. Did these ultra-rich individuals fail to make it to heaven on account of their wealth? All these great men ended their lives well in the sight of God.

Prosperity - The Dirty Word

Prosperity is neither a dirty word nor one to be avoided. I sincerely believe 'prosperity' to be one of God's favourite words because it's the embodiment of His grace. It's the central theme of the blessing conferred on Abraham by God. Believers are heirs to the blessing, which enabled Abraham prosper financially.

Yet in the recent era of church history, it has become almost abominable to preach messages bordering on financial prosperity. The few teachers and ministers of the gospel, who dare to do so, are tagged as 'prosperity preachers'. As you well know this is a tag pregnant with insinuations.

Whenever a minister of the Gospel is labeled as a prosperity preacher, it's often accompanied by veiled accusations of graft. Consequently, some ministers genuinely blessed by their faith in the gospel that births prosperity, have been labeled as 'con men'. Regrettably, this 'anti prosperity' campaign appears to be championed more by those within the Body of Christ than those without.

Those engaged in this campaign range from ordinary church members to ministers in the church. I don't deny the existence of ministers who subvert the Word of God for their personal gain. But that shouldn't prevent anyone from preaching and teaching about the riches inherent in Christ Jesus. Financial prosperity is a fundamental part of the package of salvation.

Financial prosperity is a blessing from God and should not be despised. I'm a staunch believer and 'propagator' of the gospel that includes financial prosperity. And I make no apologies for it because my position is based on Scripture.

3 John 1:2

Beloved I pray that you may prosper in all things

And be in health just as your soul prospers

It's God's will that His children prosper. Wealth is very much part of the Gospel of Jesus Christ. No one should seek to hold back that portion of the gospel from people. Anyone who purposefully excludes financial prosperity from the gospel is unconsciously doing the devil's bidding. Keeping people in poverty is the devil's agenda. Therefore, anyone contributing indirectly to that agenda is helping to promote it.

Not too long ago, there were people who believed the church to be the rightful home of poverty. This belief was underscored by the expression - 'as poor as a church mouse'. The expression sought to depict the church as the natural dwelling place of poverty. How disrespectful! I consider that an insult to God.

How can anyone seriously consider this outrageous assertion as truth? Is God not the source and creator of all wealth and riches? How can the owner and creator of wealth purposefully withhold it from His children and members of His household?

This perverted view of the church as the citadel of paucity is quite unfortunate. It's even more disappointing to see and hear Christians align with this position. All this has contributed to prosperity becoming a 'forbidden' word in the church. As a result prosperity only gets a 'respectable' mention when it's made in relation to anything else but financial well being.

I agree prosperity does not only pertain to wealth. But prosperity DOES NOT EXCLUDE wealth. The view that seeks to exclude wealth from prosperity is a deception manufactured from the devil's falsehood factory.

It's not a view emanating from God. But unfortunately, several people in the Body of Christ have docilely conformed to it. And a number of ministers have been cowed into submission as a result. Therefore, they only make feeble references to financial prosperity 'apologetically' in their sermons. They are quick to explain their use of the word 'prosperity' due to the fear of being tagged with the 'prosperity preacher' label.

Thankfully, there are a few ministers who are prepared to preach the true gospel that includes financial prosperity at the expense of their reputations. We should be bold to reject wholesale capitulation to ignorance and religious encumbrances.

The antagonism against prosperity has played a role in the poor state many of God's children find themselves in. Wealth won't become a friend or companion to you if you despise her. Jesus, though rich became poor, so that you through His poverty might become rich. Poverty was one of the things Jesus died to end in your life.

Poverty Is Not A Ticket To Heaven

Financial prosperity is of God. You don't gain automatic entry into heaven on the back of poverty and a miserable life on earth. Neither do you become an automatic candidate for hell because you are rich and wealthy.

Poverty is not a badge of honour for the believer and neither is wealth a crown of condemnation – It's time we bury this myth and put it to rest forever.

I don't believe the religious Christians who profess to 'hate' wealth really do. It's more likely a psychological adjustment they've made to justify and accept the poor state of their finances. Because they don't have money, they profess to hate it, so they will not miss it. 'If you don't have it, hate it so you don't miss it'. That in my opinion is what is going on.

Poverty is not a ticket to heaven; so don't buy into that deception. Poverty is an instrument of the devil to make your life miserable here on earth. However it appears some in the Body of Christ have bought into this deception. But it's about time the opponents of prosperity and friends of poverty realize the harm they are causing the Body of Christ. Money is not evil. The use of money by people for evil is what gives rise to the false perception of money being evil.

The only one who rejoices over the presence of poverty in the Body of Christ is the devil. The propaganda war against prosperity is a crusade orchestrated by the devil. Regrettably some Christians have unknowingly signed up as 'foot soldiers' in this crusade being waged against the children of God.

The views expressed on this issue by no means constitute an effort to condemn or impugn the integrity of anyone. I only seek to put things in the right perspective. The truth we should live by is that God is not against prosperity. Financial prosperity is the creation of God and not that of man. Man comes into this world with nothing and leaves with nothing. If this is not proof that all wealth belongs to God, I don't know what else is.

Abraham was an extremely wealthy man and his seed inherited the blessing that was imputed to him through Christ Jesus. If you belong to Christ, then you are Abraham's seed, and an heir to the exceedingly great and precious promises of God.

Galatians 3:29

And if you are Christ's

Then you are Abraham's seed

And heirs according to the promise

The promise made to Abraham was to his seed as well. You're the seed of Abraham through Christ Jesus and therefore an heir of that blessing. You are the beneficiary of the covenant between God and Abraham. Prosperity in all things, including financial prosperity is your birthright. Embrace it, acknowledge it and live in the reality of it. Hallelujah!!!

Chapter Five

Poverty Is Not A Blessing

There should be no doubt in anybody's mind that poverty is not and can't be a virtue. It's a condition of life that should be rejected and not embraced. Poverty is a significant contributor to the suffering in the world. Poverty primarily accounts for the increasing numbers of people who risk their lives journeying across deserts and oceans from the poorer parts of the world in search of greener pastures.

Poverty should not be engaged, encouraged or tolerated in the life of the child of God. It's an oppressive spirit and a vicious beast. It has no place in the life of the believer of Christ Jesus and shouldn't be romanticized as a godly trait. It has nothing resembling God in it. God is love but poverty certainly isn't. It destroys one's ability to love.

This beast called poverty has not been a source of blessing for anybody I know of. It only brings misery and hardship into the lives of those overcome by it. Poverty is a tool used by the devil to destroy lives in much the same way sickness does. That's what it is and should be recognized as.

Marriages and families are failing and falling apart because of overwhelming financial insufficiency challenges and issues. There are many unhappy homes and families because the money available is not enough to meet their pressing daily needs and requirements.

Financial insufficiency takes away the self-respect and confidence of a man. It turns him into a 'cowering chicken' instead of the bold lion God created him to be. Poverty destroys the trust and security a wife needs to place in her husband as the breadwinner and head of the home. It facilitates 'premature independence' in the family setting, which often produces wayward children.

When children are forced to provide for themselves what their parents should have provided for them, bad things do happen. They cease to be children and are forced to fend for themselves like adults. Under these circumstances young girls are compelled to engage in prostitution as a means of providing for themselves. And teenage boys resort to armed robbery and homosexuality to procure what their parents can't provide.

Financially strapped married and unmarried women become victims of unscrupulous rich men on a regular basis because of their poor financial situation. In some instances the reverse is the case with financially well-placed women exploiting men without means. Due to poverty mothers and wives are forced to provide for their families by 'any means necessary'. This includes providing certain 'favours' to men other than their husbands in return for money. Husbands and fathers are unable to be good husbands and fathers because they are 'crippled' financially and are unable to play these roles effectively.

Again, because of financial insufficiency, aging parents fail to receive the care and attention due them from their grown children. This situation arises because the financial means to provide care doesn't exist. It can be quite embarrassing for a grown child who is unable to financially support his or her aging parents.

I have had personal experience with financial insufficiency and it isn't pleasant. It is fraught with many painful and embarrassing moments. I can remember occasions I really wanted to be a blessing to my parents and loved ones, but I couldn't afford to do so. Even your ability to be a supportive family member is limited because of poverty. How can poverty be a good thing?

When you're caught in the vicious claws of poverty you can forget about becoming the favourite uncle or aunt of your nieces and nephews. Children thrive on presents and surprises. But if you're not well resourced financially how could you possibly be a blessing to these young ones you love so much?

There are people who look much older than their age because of the financial situation they find themselves in. Poverty has added lines to their faces and 'years' to their ages. They only smile and laugh on a few precious occasions because poverty doesn't give one many things to laugh about. People have become sick with heart related ailments due to the financial lack in their lives and the pressures it comes with.

Poverty is harmful and should not be countenanced in any measure. You should reject and resist poverty with all your strength in Christ Jesus. Reject the myths and deception of the devil with respect to wealth. Build yourself up with the Word of Grace and obtain your financial inheritance in Christ Jesus.

Chapter Six
Poverty Is Not A Rite Of Passage

There is a belief held by some in the Body of Christ that poverty is a rite of passage. According to this viewpoint 'true' believers will more than likely experience poverty in their lifetime. They consider poverty is a rite of passage believers must endure to 'qualify' for God's blessing. It appears to be a popularly held belief, but it's inconsistent with everything Jesus Christ represents and sacrificed His life on the cross for.

Poverty can't be described as a rite of passage for the child of God by any stretch of the imagination. The finished works of Christ guarantees that. He took away poverty from you and unto Himself. Then He gave you His wealth in return. He didn't 'refine' it and give it back to you to bear.

2 Corinthians 8:9

For you know the grace of our Lord Jesus Christ

That though He was rich

Yet for your sakes He became poor

That you through His poverty might become rich

The exchange by Jesus of His wealth for your poverty was part of the payment He made to secure your redemption. To describe poverty as a 'rite of passage' for the believer, is as good as declaring the works of Jesus unfinished. Jesus finished what He came to do over two thousand years ago. Meaning your repositioning from the darkness of poverty to the light of financial sufficiency was accomplished two thousand years ago.

The Wilderness Experience Poverty Doctrine

I believe with all due respect that the 'poverty as a rite of passage' doctrine is propagated primarily by Christians who experienced financial hardship in the early stages of their walk with God. They believe God orchestrated the period of lack in their lives, in order to inculcate in them a sense of dependence on Him.

Consequently, the experience of financial hardship has been adopted by them as doctrine. I call it the 'wilderness experience poverty doctrine'. This doctrine has seemingly become the 'economic standard' they subscribe to and live by. On the face of it, the doctrine sounds reasonable. However, it flies in the face of the underlying principle of the New Covenant, which is PROVISION. Under the New Covenant God provides as a sign of His love. He does not withhold or make poor.

At every stage of the relationship between God and man He has always provided, He does not withhold. He's the recognized provider, hence the name 'Jehovah Jireh' – the Lord will provide. God provided His Son as the sacrificial lamb to save mankind, at the time the world had sinned and deserved punishment. God did not withhold His Son. In providing His Son, God provided everything and held nothing back. Everything including financial sufficiency and wealth are vested in His Son.

Now that you have been justified by the Blood of Jesus you have been saved from wrath through Him. The consequences of God's wrath are encapsulated in the Curse of the Law, which includes the affliction of poverty. But the Blood of Christ has neutralized the effects of the curse on your finances.

Romans 5:8 - 9

But God demonstrates His own love toward us

In that while we still sinners, Christ died for us

Much more then, having now been justified by His blood

We shall be saved from wrath through Him

John 3:16

For God so loved the world that He gave His only begotten Son

That whoever believes in Him should not perish

But have everlasting life

God gave up His Son so you and I wouldn't perish through poverty but have everlasting life. Poverty cannot be synonymous with everlasting life. Everlasting life connotes a good life, a blessed life. Not a ride through the 'wilderness of poverty'.

Once justified by the Blood of Jesus you are saved from enduring poverty as a rite of passage. Poverty can in no way be recognized as a rite of passage for the child of God.

On many occasions I've heard ministers of God uphold their time in 'financial wilderness' as a badge of honour. For them it's a necessary experience in order to become a 'seasoned' child of God. They even go ahead to claim one can't become a true minister of God without experiencing poverty.

With all due respect, I strongly and fervently disagree with this position. I can't find any New Testament scripture that supports the assertion that a true disciple of Christ Jesus must experience poverty in order to be approved by Him. Jesus died to make you rich and not poor.

It's undeniable that a number of ministers of God come from poor to modest to financial backgrounds. Consequently some of them experienced tough and rough times in the early days of their ministry work. Testimonies and biographies of several ministers attest to this fact.

Eventually, as they obtained insight into the Word of God and increased in knowledge, their circumstances changed for the better. They matured into 'sonship' and became rightful heirs and partakers of the blessings of their Heavenly Father. Their new insight and understanding moved them from financial insufficiency to abundant supply.

However, some of these ministers can't seem to link their blessing with their maturity in the knowledge of the Word. They think and believe it was the plan of God for them to suffer lack and hardship as a prelude to being blessed by Him. That can't be right because the New Testament doesn't support this assertion.

Life Experience Is Not Doctrine

The general acceptance of the wilderness experience as doctrine exemplifies the occasional metamorphosis of negative life experiences into doctrine. This is a religious trait and shouldn't be allowed to corrupt the doctrine of Christ.

This is not to say life experiences have no place in teaching the Word of God because they do. However, when you illustrate your teaching with life experiences, they should line up exactly with the principles and message of the Gospel of Christ. The illustration should affirm and not be 'almost the same' as the Word of God. There are no parallel truths when it comes to the Word of God.

You can't claim poverty is a rite of passage based on Scripture just because that's what you experienced. In much the same way you can't say being childless is the will of God for some people because you don't have children yourself. We are called believers because we believe in the Gospel of Jesus Christ as the only truth. We don't subscribe to a gospel borne of our own personal experiences.

Testimonies are accounts of the personal experiences of people who have faced some challenges in their lives. But testimonies testify to the validity and infallibility of the Word of God. Personal experiences that appear to provide 'alternative facts' to what the Word of God has explicitly declared can't be accepted as supporting Scripture.

A life of poverty is not a true testament of the Gospel of Jesus Christ. It's in total contradiction to it. The 'wilderness experience' theory in relation to poverty goes against the grain of the Gospel of Jesus Christ. It's more a religious based doctrine and not a truth founded on the grace of God.

I disagree with the acceptance of the wilderness experience in the Body of Christ. This doctrine has 'facilitated' the tolerance of poverty by believers. They have bought into the belief that the wilderness experience is 'ordained' by God and in line with His will for their lives.

God does not want anyone to go through suffering before 'qualifying' for a blessing. The suffering of Jesus took care of all suffering. God only wants you to know what you are entitled to!!! Once you get to know what belongs to you, He wants you to have it. Hallelujah!!!

The Myth Of Suffering For Christ

Poverty is not synonymous with suffering for Christ. This is a myth and a deception from hell's falsehood factory. It's desperate attempt by the devil to make poverty 'respectable'. But instead of suffering for Christ, we make Jesus 'suffer' when our lives reflect poverty. When believers live in poverty it suggests His sacrifice was meaningless and of no benefit.

The suffering of Jesus was meant to be the ultimate suffering on behalf of all mankind. No additional suffering or sacrifice is required or needed. Jesus did it all and there is no more work to be done by anyone. Jesus affirms this when He declared on the cross that it was finished!!! Accept what Jesus achieved with His sacrifice and enjoy the fruits of the sacrifice. IT IS FINISHED!! The suffering has run its course.

John 19:30

So when Jesus had received the sour wine

He said, 'It is finished'

And bowing His head, He gave up His spirit

Poverty is finished. You don't have to be poor any longer. Jesus does not appreciate you enduring poverty because of Him and does not want to see it. Jesus doesn't require or regard poverty as a sign of your commitment or devotion to Him.

Hebrews 12:2

Looking unto Jesus, the author and finisher of our faith

Who for the joy that was set before Him endured the cross

Despising the shame and has sat down at right hand of the throne of God

The joy that was set before Him on the cross was the joy of seeing poverty come to an end in your life. The joy was not caused by seeing poverty coming to life in your circumstances. That's why though He is rich; He became poor, so that you might become rich in Him.

2 Corinthians 8:9

For you know the grace of our Lord Jesus Christ

That though He was rich, yet for your sakes He became poor

That you through His poverty might become rich

This notion of suffering for Christ, I believe exists because of two main reasons. The first reason is 'religion'. For religiously minded people poverty is a sign of 'holiness'. In their view holiness is synonymous with hardship, which they incorrectly believe to be pleasing to God.

Some even believe suffering physically as a result of financial insufficiency is a pathway to 'spiritual purity'. There is nothing spiritually pure about being poor. Our father Abraham was a wealthy man by all standards, perhaps the richest man in his time on earth. However, Abraham was not accused of being spiritually deficient or lacking in righteousness because of his immense wealth.

On the contrary, God commended him for his righteousness. Therefore, there is nothing to the 'religious' belief that suffering in poverty is pleasing to God. It's not and can't be. It doesn't make you the apple of His eye.

The need for the psychological justification of poverty is the second reason people subscribe to the 'suffering for Christ' myth. People engage in the psychological justification of poverty to help them mentally accept their depressing financial circumstances.

People who find themselves in this boat know they are poor and hate the fact that they are poor. However, due to their inability to find a way out, they conjure 'acceptable' reasons to justify their poor financial status. The reasons range from comical to the absurd and include.

1. The rich have no peace so I would rather be poor.

2. It is not God's will for me to be rich that is why I am poor.

3. My wealth is in heaven and not on earth.

4. This earth is not my home, I am only passing through

Quite clearly, these reasons lack any scriptural basis. They are only feeble attempts by people to assuage their dismal financial state. In the end it still does not make any kind of sense for the redeemed child of God to live with the 'trappings' of poverty.

It's not in the nature of God to approve of the needless suffering of His children. If human beings deem it good to bless their children, will God who sacrificed His Son for mankind not give more?

Poverty brings untold misery into the lives of those affected by it. That can't be what God stands for and certainly not what Jesus died on the cross for. God's will is for you to prosper financially and that should be your expectation for your life also.

The Divine Rite of Passage

A believer destiny according to Scripture is to live through a divine rite of passage and not a 'poverty ridden rite of passage.

2 Corinthians 9:8

And God is able to make all grace abound toward you

That you, always having all sufficiency in all things

Will have an abundance for every good work

God created and planned for you to ALWAYS have sufficiency in ALL THINGS. You are NOT meant to lack anything. You are ordained to be sufficient in everything all the time. You're not meant to be lacking in anything during your time on earth. That is the definition of the divine rite of passage. You are not supposed to lack money. You are not predestined to experience penury as part of the 'initiation rites' into the Kingdom of God.

You have been set up and programmed by God to have everything and lack nothing. The divine rite of passage is what you are supposed to experience and not the wilderness experience of financial insufficiency. Reject any doctrine that champions poverty in your life. It can't be from God.

Chapter Seven

Financial Insufficiency Is A Choice

Based on what Christ has accomplished, living in poverty has to be by choice for the believer. You cannot be poor after becoming one with Christ Jesus. You can't be poor unless you choose to be poor.

The basis for becoming a child of God and a citizen of the Kingdom of God is your spiritual union with Christ. After this spiritual union you can only be poor or experience financial insufficiency because you choose to. The spiritual union is a total and complete fusion of everything that pertains to your life with that of Christ Jesus.

You have ceased to exist as an ordinary individual. Everything about you has been transformed to conform to that of Christ. Your finances have also been transformed to conform to the finances of Christ. This is the spiritual reality of becoming one with Christ. Your life and your finances are inextricably linked to that of Christ Jesus.

At this stage it is your choice either to live as a rich poor person or live the life your spiritual union with Christ has birthed. If you are a believer and poor, it is equivalent to someone having money in the bank and choosing not to access it.

Don't resign yourself to a life of penury. If you find yourself in the cycle of financial insufficiency you can come out of it. Give your attention to Christ and what He's done to make you rich. Meditate on scriptures that proclaim this truth and see your circumstances change before your eyes.

There are people who claim they would rather be poor and go to heaven than be rich and miss out on heaven. Well, first of all, paucity does not guarantee you a place in heaven. Secondly heaven is not the preserve of the poor. It's therefore a terrible choice to opt for a life of penury so you can get to heaven.

Nobody ought to live in the fear of being condemned to hell because they are wealthy. Wealth does not cause you to sin or reject Christ. Wealth merely amplifies and reveals who you really are. It amplifies what is good in you as well what is bad about an individual if any.

A few people 'lose their heads' when they become wealthy. But wealth does not automatically enroll people in the 'Pride & Arrogance Academy'. Losing your head over money is a function and failure of character. It is not a consequence of wealth.

Some people masquerade and present themselves as humble and God-fearing folk until they become rich. Suddenly on becoming rich, the humble and God-fearing person you knew becomes a proud and overbearingly arrogant person. This is what has led to a generalization that wealth corrupts people.

Wealth doesn't always transform previously humble individuals into proud and arrogant people. Any arrogance that is exhibited may have already been present but hidden because there was no medium of expression. But hidden pride and arrogance can wake up from hibernation because wealth provides them an avenue of expression.

If an individual is humble, their humility will be revealed and amplified by wealth. On the other hand, if their heart is full of pride and arrogance that's what will be projected for all to see. Nobody ought to shun prosperity because they are wary they will 'ooze' pride once they become rich.

To shun prosperity is a choice open to you, but one I urge you not to make. The fear of wealth is a fear tactic employed by the devil to drive you into poverty. The fear of anything emanates from the devil. Refuse his invitation to lure you into the bondage of fear and poverty from which Christ has set you free.

Galatians 5:1

Stand fast therefore in the liberty by which Christ has made us free

And do not be entangled again with a yoke of bondage

Respect The Blessing of Prosperity

Every believer should learn to respect the blessing of prosperity and not deride it. Derision will repel your prosperity because you only attract what you respect. You attract the blessing of prosperity by affirming its manifestation in your life with the Word of God. Therefore if you respect the blessing of God you will attract it into your life.

The manifestation of prosperity in your life may have to 'activated'. The manifestation of prosperity is not necessarily automatic. You activate your financial prosperity using the Word of God, your faith and your seed.

Believe the Word by faith, sow it as seed and affirm it in your life to reap whatever you need. You may sow the Word as seed with an offering if you are led by the Holy Spirit to do so. Endeavour to seek guidance from the Holy Spirit when you sow because the end result is unique for everybody. The Holy Spirit is the Spirit of Truth and knows what you seek to know and where to find it.

In my book 'Living Under The Influence', I talk extensively about the correct mechanics of effectively confessing the Word of God. The Word of God should be meaningfully confessed and not recited like a nursery rhyme without any conviction. When you confess and declare the Word of God with conviction, you affirm what God has already achieved for you.

Ultimately prosperity is a matter of choice because you have been made rich in Christ Jesus and your money is already in the bank. Hallelujah. The decision whether or not to make a 'withdrawal' through verbal acknowledgements and confession is entirely up to you.

Poverty Is A False Reality

Poverty in the life a believer is a false reality and should be recognized as such. The true reality is that you are rich in Christ Jesus. Poverty in the life of a believer is 'ungodly'. It's not the true state of affairs as ordained by God. Poverty is a mirage created by the devil, but can become a living reality if you tolerate and accept it.

2 Corinthians 8:9
For you know the grace of our Lord Jesus Christ
That though He was rich
Yet for your sakes He became poor
That you through His poverty
Might become rich

You have been made a joint heir with Christ to the riches and glory of your Heavenly Father. Your relationship with your Heavenly Father alone 'qualifies' you as a rich person. I'm yet to see or hear of an acknowledged child of a billionaire being described as poor even though the child may not have legally inherited the wealth of the parents just yet. In most, if not all instances, the children of rich parents are described as 'rich kids'. They are acknowledged as rich and are rich because of their relationship to wealthy parents.

If being related to a mere mortal can qualify one as rich, how then should the child of God be described? Your Heavenly Father is the Originator and Creator of all wealth. He owns the whole world and everything in it. Don't forget in Heaven where He lives, the streets are paved with gold.

The simple truth is that every born again believer is a rich kid in reality. You are rich because your Father is rich. Your Heavenly Father is also the owner of all wealth. This is the true state of the believer. However, your wealth is a spiritual reality that must be believed and acknowledged before it becomes a tangible reality in your life.

It is the plan and wish of God that His children prosper in all things including prospering financially.

3 John 1:2
Beloved, I pray that you may prosper in all things
And be in health, just as your soul prospers

Chapter Eight
Slaves of Prosperity

Poverty is a fruit of the sinful nature. Therefore if you have been set free from sin and the fruit of sin, you have been set free fro m poverty also. Righteousness is the opposite of the sinful nature. Therefore, having been set free from sin is to be delivered into righteousness.

Romans 6:18

And having been set free from sin

You became slaves of righteousness

When you were a slave to sin, you were also a slave to the fruit of sin. Poverty is a fruit of sin and being a slave to sin meant, poverty was indirectly your master. In other words you were under the dominion of poverty.

But when you are in spiritual union with Christ you become a slave of righteousness. Financial prosperity is a fruit of the righteousness Christ makes available. Therefore, financial prosperity becomes your 'master' by default. If you are a slave of righteousness, you can also be described as being under the dominion of financial prosperity. Hallelujah!!

If you are under the dominion of financial prosperity, financial insufficiency shouldn't be the status quo in your life. You should never entertain the thought of being broke or experiencing lack. It's as far away from you as the heavens are from the earth. It's a reality only you can cause to manifest in your life.

The sinful nature pertains to the life and character of a person under the dominion of sin and in 'good standing' with the devil. Righteousness on the other hand pertains to the nature of one in right-standing with God. When you are in right-standing with God, a fruit of that right-standing relationship you should experience is financial prosperity.

Slaves of Righteousness

Scripture describes all those who have yielded their hearts to the Lordship and ownership of God through Christ Jesus as slaves of righteousness. The definition of a slave is one owned by another and whose life is subject to the owner's volition. The slave is also described as one who has lost the power of resistance and surrenders to something.

The depiction of believers as slaves of righteousness highlights their liberation from the bondage of sin (the devil) and the 'evil dividends' of sin that includes poverty. It also underlines the ownership of their lives and destinies by God after their redemption with the Blood of Jesus.

1 Corinthians 6:20

For you were bought at a price

Therefore glorify God in your body and in your spirit, which are God's

Romans 6:18, 22

And having been set free from sin, you became slaves of righteousness

But now having been set free from sin, and having become slaves of God

You have your fruit to holiness and the end everlasting life

As a slave of righteousness your life is subject to the volition of God. Meaning only God determines the outcomes in your life. What happens in your life is subject only to the will of God, since you are His 'slave'. Once God makes you rich in Christ Jesus (2 Corinthians 8:9) nothing or no one can change that.

Being a slave of righteousness also means you are the bonafide property of God. Legally when somebody owns something, no other person has the right to tamper with the property in question. Since God owns you the devil has no right or power to tamper with your life and finances.

Yet another definition of a slave, describes a slave as one who has lost the power of resistance and surrenders to something. Consequently, as a slave of righteousness you have lost the power to resist the righteousness of God and its attendant blessings. You have for all intents and purposes 'succumbed' to the blessing of God. You are subject to the wealth of God even if you don't ask for it.

To be declared a slave of righteousness means you have been declared a slave of prosperity. Prosperity is a fruit of righteousness. Therefore, once you attain right-standing with God; prosperity becomes a by-product of that fellowship. You are a 'slave of God's blessings'. It means God's blessings come upon you whether you want them to or not. You don't have a say in this, because you are a 'slave'. Hallelujah!!

Righteousness Includes Prosperity

When righteousness is imputed on an individual the seed of prosperity is planted in the individual as well. So poverty only remains a choice for a child of God blessed with the seed of prosperity. But whether you decide to nurture your seed of prosperity to fruition is a choice only you can make for yourself. Every child of God has received the grace to be prosperous. Financial insufficiency is not the ordained way of life for any believer. Financial prosperity is the ordained way.

More can be done to advance the Kingdom of God and help people through financial prosperity than poverty ever could. Reject the deception of the devil that says it is acceptable to be poor. It is stressful and humiliating to be poor and that is no life for a child of God.

Poverty should not be tolerated and accommodated. Everybody is a solution to somebody and to something. We are uniquely created for unique purposes. Your prosperity will manifest following how well you provide solutions to the problems you are uniquely gifted to solve.

Your diligence and efficiency in solving problems will provide a demand for your solutions. As the demand for your solutions soar, so will your value. And as your value increases, your prosperity will increasingly manifest also.

You can't look God in the face (if that were possible) and complain you are good for nothing. He uniquely created you as a unique solution. There is no way you can claim to be useless or irrelevant. You were created to address a peculiar problem so find the problem and fix it.

Light Overcomes Darkness

The devil has been quite efficient in keeping Christians in the prison of poverty for so long that it has become an acceptable way of life for many of them. The devil may have had his way for a while but the light of the Word of God must be used to overcome the darkness

The entrance of the Word of God brings illumination. The darkness of poverty can't resist or stand the light of prosperity. Financial insufficiency is a manifestation of the kingdom of darkness and it has no place in your life; it must give way.

Psalm 119:130

The entrance of Your Word gives light

It gives understanding to the simple

Chapter Nine
The Covenant Blessing Of Abraham

The Blessing of Abraham is a covenant blessing established between God and Abraham and to his seed in Christ Jesus. Scripture describes the seed of Abraham as those who have received Christ Jesus as their Lord and Saviour. If you have received Jesus as your Lord and Saviour, then you are considered the seed of Abraham through Him. Your designation as the seed of Abraham qualifies you as a beneficiary of the Abrahamic blessing.

Galatians 3:29

And if you are Christ's then you are Abraham's seed

And heirs according to the promise

This Covenant Blessing of Abraham of which you are a beneficiary is irrevocable. The blessing from the covenant is guaranteed and can't be invalidated. There is nothing you can do short of rejecting Christ that can invalidate or break the covenant. A covenant is made between two parties and in the case of the 'Abrahamic Covenant' it was between God and Abraham.

The process of invalidating a covenant must be initiated by either one or both parties involved in the covenant and not by a beneficiary of the covenant. As Abraham's seed you are a beneficiary of the Abrahamic covenant through Christ and not a party or 'signatory' to the covenant.

Thus if either God or Abraham fail to initiate the process of abrogating the Abrahamic Covenant no one else can. That's why nothing short of rejecting Christ can prevent you from benefitting from the covenant. You are a child of the covenant and not a direct party to the covenant.

A link with Christ is necessary to inherit the blessing because you can only be connected to Abraham through Christ Jesus. The New Testament believer has no direct relationship with Abraham the father of faith. So believers are only recognized as seeds of Abraham because of their spiritual union with Christ Jesus.

The Abrahamic blessing is actually the 'repackaging' of the blessing God first made available to man through the first Adam. When bestowed on you, it invokes the power of the Most High God on your behalf. It is the restoration of the original blessing God bequeathed to mankind upon creation, but revoked when Adam sinned. The blessing of Abraham is a supernatural empowering force that transcends generations and guarantees success in every endeavour and enterprise.

Genesis 12:2-3

I will make you a great nation; I will bless you and make your name great

And you will be a blessing

I will bless those who bless you and I will curse him who curses you

And in you all the families of the earth will be blessed

Galatians 3:14

That the blessing of Abraham might come upon the Gentiles in Christ Jesus

That we might receive the promise of the Spirit through faith

Let me a make a clarification here concerning the blessing of Abraham you are an heir to. You are not an heir to the physical property Abraham acquired during his lifetime. You are an heir to the 'spiritual blessing' that was bestowed upon him by God. Abraham became exceedingly and extremely rich as a result of the spiritual blessing bestowed on him.

Empowered To Succeed

You have been empowered supernaturally to prosper in all things because of the covenant blessing 'on' your life. However, this is a revelation many in the Body of Christ are yet to fully comprehend.

The covenant blessing empowers you supernaturally to succeed in whatever you put your hand to. You must be conscious of this 'blessing' and EXPECT to succeed in everything you do because of it. YOU CAN'T FAIL. Failure is not an option to be considered. The supernatural blessing enabled Isaac to sow in a time of extreme famine and reap a hundredfold harvest. This is the nature of the blessing upon your life. You have no reason or excuse to fail in anything.

Genesis 26:12-13

Then Isaac sowed in the land and reaped in the same year a hundredfold

And the Lord blessed him

The man began to prosper

And continued prospering until he became very prosperous.

Your location and the environment of your location are irrelevant to the working of the blessing. Neither does the type of business you are engaged in matter to the blessing. If the Lord approves of your business activity as He did in the case of Isaac, it shall surely prosper. Your means of generating income must be approved by God.

Make sure you have heard from God before you engage in the business. Don't be seduced by mouth-watering projections and job offers. The only reason Isaac reaped a hundredfold harvest was because he heard from God. Isaac listened to God and obeyed His instructions before sowing under those testing conditions.

Isaac must have looked foolish to the people in his community because it didn't make sense to sow at the time he did. He did so when everybody else was moving to seek 'greener' pastures elsewhere. He must have faced opposition even from his family members and close associates regarding his decision to stay put as God had advised him to. But Isaac had consulted with God and because he did, he reaped an improbable harvest; a harvest supernaturally facilitated by God.

How To Activate The Blessing

The Abrahamic Blessing is activated by first acknowledging the power of Good to bless you. Then verbally affirm the power of 'The Blessing' on yourself and on the project. While doing this you must position yourself spiritually to receive the wisdom and guidance of .God on the project.

You position yourself spiritually by engaging in prayer, worship and meditation on the Word of God. Meditate on scriptures that talk about the blessings of God. It's important that you stay sensitive so you don't miss God's promptings

Proverbs 3:5-6

Trust in the Lord with all your heart and lean not on your own understanding

In all your ways acknowledge Him and He shall direct your paths

Don't expect to physically 'feel' the blessing because you probably won't. You live your life as a child of God, based on the knowledge of God's Word and not on your feelings. You will not physically feel the blessing, but you know it's part of you based on your knowledge of the Word. Engage the Holy Spirit to help order your steps and direct your paths. He's the Spirit of Truth. He knows exactly what you're supposed to do and when to do it.

The only reason you may not have seen 'the blessing' working for you yet is because you may have failed to switch it on. Your belief, verbal confessions and acknowledgment of the blessing are what activates it. Once activated, it won't be long before you see the manifestation of the 'blessing' in your circumstances.

Engaging the blessing is not synonymous with 'begging for alms'. Therefore your confessions shouldn't amount to wailing and begging God to come to your rescue. You are a child of the covenant therefore every blessing vested in it is already yours. You're only supposed to AFFIRM not cry and beg for something already yours. God is not a man to go back on His Word. The blessing is GUARANTEED.

Many of us can attest to missed opportunities and botched projects because of our failure to consult God beforehand. We can also point to business plans that went awry as a consequence of disregarding God's advice. But in some instances of failure it could be God closing one door in order to open a bigger door. It behoves you to be spiritually sensitive to discern and adhere to the advice of God.

Business plans and ventures go awry because people fail to engage 'the blessing'. When the blessing is fully engaged and working, failure does not stand a chance.

Chapter Ten
You Have Power To Get Wealth

God the creator of the heavens and the earth, has given you POWER to get wealth. Everything necessary for the manifestation of your wealth is in place. You have been divinely set up to be rich if you so desire.

Deuteronomy 8:18

And you shall remember the Lord your God

For it is He who gives you POWER to get wealth

That He may establish His covenant which He swore to your fathers

As it is this day.

Because God has ordained it, no opposition against the manifestation of your wealth will prevail. If God, the creator of the heavens and earth has given you the POWER to get wealth, who or what could possibly prevent your wealth from manifestation? Who can reverse your destiny established in Christ? Your financial prosperity has been divinely established and it's not reversible.

Isaiah 43:13

Indeed, before the day was, I am He

And there is no one who can deliver out of my hand

I work and who will reverse it?

Your wealth has been reserved in Christ awaiting your retrieval of it. Don't see yourself as poor and striving to be rich. The blessing on your life is a done deal and requires no special prayers from you. It's an inheritance and a divine empowerment from God to all who believe in Jesus as their Lord and Saviour.

The essence of divine empowerment is that divine assistance has been put at your disposal. That means you have the resources and influence of God working on your behalf to ensure success in your endeavours.

Now imagine doing business, with God's influence and resources working on your behalf. I'm sure you would walk with more than a spring in your step. It is more likely you would walk with a 'rocket launcher' in your step. This is the reality of the believer and it is not a hypothetical scenario. You should walk in the consciousness of God's awesome power actively working on your behalf. Hallelujah!!

You no longer have to put your trust and confidence in men no matter how highly placed they are. Here today, gone tomorrow is the way with all men. All men, no matter how influential or powerful, are like grass - they wither and die. God is the only One whose existence is guaranteed, thus worthy of your trust and hope.

Sometimes Christians behave as though having God on their side is not enough. As a result they permit adverse financial situations that confront them to be transformed through fear into monsters that can't be tamed. They make God appear 'small' in relation to their challenges. God has given you power to get wealth and that is all you need. It is more than enough. No man is capable of adding anything to your life. You don't need anything extra from a man to succeed and prosper when you have Christ.

Effect Change To Create Wealth

Wealth is created by causing change in the way things are done for the better. By virtue of your divine empowerment, you have the ability to cause change in a place or situation to create wealth for yourself in the process.

But there are believers who rule themselves out of becoming financially prosperous due to the circumstances of their birth and location. In their estimation, the probability of them becoming wealthy is less than that of building a house on the sun.

But true believers should realize the power of God in the believer to cause change is not limited by birth parents or by the location. You may have been born in the middle of the desert, but that can't constitute a limitation. There is no situation that is beyond God. Your situation and circumstances can't challenge God's ability to provide a solution through you. Every situation is firmly within His control and ability to change it for the better through you. God has placed the power to create and provide solutions in everyone. You have the ability to effect change and provide solutions whenever it is needed. The solutions you provide are what will create wealth for you.

The resources of God at your disposal include human, financial capital, business expertise and the wisdom to put it all together. It includes everything you will ever need to create wealth for yourself. You can't fail in your effort to create wealth for yourself.

Deuteronomy 28:8, 12

The Lord will command His blessings on you in your storehouses

And in all you set your hand

And He will bless you in the land which the Lord your God is giving you

The Lord will open to you His good treasure

The heavens to give the rain to your land in its season

And to bless all the work of your hand

You shall lend to many nations but you shall not borrow

Chapter Eleven
God Teaches You To Profit

God teaches you to profit. He leads you by the way you should go and the business ideas to pursue. Every believer should see God as his or her 'business development and marketing consultant'. In that capacity God can guide you on the business direction and ideas to pursue if you allow Him to. If God is your 'consultant' your business will not fail or make losses.

Isaiah 48:17

Thus says the Lord, your Redeemer, the Holy One of Israel

I am the Lord your God Who teaches you to profit

Who leads you by the way you should go.

I describe the dire financial challenges of believers as 'false poverty' because no believer is poor in reality. Indigence is not a true reflection of who and what the believer is. The believer is a joint heir of God with Christ Jesus. And an heir of God CANNOT be poor. For a believer to be considered poor is like saying the sun emits darkness instead of light. The sun does not emit darkness and a believer can't be poor.

No believer should live in fear of his or her business failing to make a profit. If God is in the business there should be no such fear. God teaches and leads you to profit. God does not teach and lead you to lose. Just because you face challenges in your business does not mean God is not with you. Challenges may come, but take heart because they were overcome even before they began.

Christ overcame all challenges on your behalf. Therefore, challenges have only one outcome where you're concerned – they always end in your favour. All things have been designed by God 'to work together' for your good. You always have victory in Christ Jesus. Sometimes when you seek God's help in the middle of a challenge, the effects of the challenge appear to persist in spite of your prayers before their resolution. That's the reason God reminds us not to be afraid so many times in the Bible. Fear not because victory will ultimately be yours.

When you stand firm and exercise unwavering faith, God's Word in the long run will come to pass. Learn to speak things that are not as though they exist just as your Heavenly Father does. Let your confessions reflect God's Word of victory and not the adverse staring you in the face. Praise God.

When God speaks, He sees and speaks the end from the beginning. In other words He doesn't see your adversity; He only sees your victory over the adversity. God doesn't live in the realm of adversity so He doesn't consider that as reality.

God lives in the realm of victory according to His Word. Victory is His only reality because all circumstances are within His control. Nothing can overpower or overwhelm Him. Likewise for the believer, victory is your true reality. No circumstance should overwhelm you.

Jesus tells us to be of good cheer because He has delivered us from the power of darkness. Poverty is a manifestation of the power of darkness. From the Word of God we know Jesus overcame poverty and the other elements of the world that oppose believers, in His resurrection.

Colossians 2:15

He has delivered us from the power of darkness

And translated us into the Kingdom of the Son of His love

Luke 10:19

Behold, I give you the authority to trample on serpents and scorpions

And over all the power of the enemy and nothing shall by any means hurt you

Jesus has delivered you from poverty and given you the authority to overcome it. You have divine authority to reject poverty in any form or manifestation. Don't 'manage' or live with financial insufficiency. In Christ, you have overcome the elements of the world that seek to prevent you from experiencing financial freedom. Put your total and absolute trust in the Lord.

Abraham did not consider the 'liabilities' of his old body when he was told he would have a child. Like Abraham did refuse to consider any 'liabilities' connected to your business. Consider the challenges God's to overcome not yours. Cast all your burdens upon Him and claim ownership of none.

The work of ensuring you make profit takes place in the realm of the spirit where God reigns. The spirit realm is where your focus should be and not in the physical realm where the challenges appear to manifest. Focus on the spiritual realities that are not seen with optical eyes (2 Corinthians 4:18).

Continue to engage the Word of God. When you engage the Word, you disengage from prevailing challenges. Don't look at the things that are seen. Let the One (God) in charge of all things lead you by the way you should go.

In the Bible, we learn that Isaac (Abraham's son) considered joining the bandwagon to Egypt because of a severe famine that had descended on the land. But God instructed him to remain where he was. Isaac believed God in spite of the contrary conditions he could see and experienced. He believed the Word of God and Almighty God did not disappoint.

I'm sure Isaac was misunderstood when he continued farming under drought conditions instead of joining the bandwagon to Egypt. But he trusted in God and obeyed the instruction for him to stay where he was. He provided God an opportunity to show up and be God and did God show up!!

Isaac reaped a hundred fold harvest of what he sowed and went on to become exceedingly wealthy. Believing the Word of God in the middle of the 'raging storm' poses a challenge for many Christians. Many of us have not yet come to the place where we live by what the Word says. We live by what they see and how they feel.

The Christian life is a knowledge-based existence. This implies your life should be based on what you know in Christ and not on what you think or feel. Christianity is a 'knowledge and not a feeling'. Don't follow the example of people who fail to consult God, prior to taking decisions. Then when things start to unravel, they try belatedly to enlist God in their plans.

Overcomers In Christ

Whatever is born of God overcomes the world. Since you are born of God, so are the business ventures you engage in. If you make God part of your business endeavours they will surely overcome any adversary and the competition.

1 John 5:4

For whatever is born of God overcomes the world

And this is the victory that has overcome the world; our faith.

Businesses in many parts of the world face tremendous challenges that put their survival at risk. The challenges are many and varied. But if you're a child of God you're immune to adverse challenges because your endeavours are born of God. Your endeavours will survive and overcome like Isaac overcame the severe famine that threatened to destroy his farming business

A business that is born of God should be one in which you engage in nothing untoward and can boldly invite God to be part. You can't possess the nature of God and be engaged in a business that bears no resemblance to the nature and character of God. The character of Christ should reflect in your business dealings.

Don't start a business or be invited into one based solely on the advice and recommendation of men. Men are mere mortals with no definite knowledge of future events and prospects. They can only provide an 'educated' guess based on their limited human expertise and knowledge.

But there is someone - the Almighty God who has definite knowledge of the future. He knows the future because He created it. Hallelujah!! He's the one you ought to believe and trust in. He knows the past, the present and the future. He can even change the past to profit your future because He's not limited by time. He teaches you to profit and leads you by the way you should go. With Him by your side you can't fail or miss the mark.

Chapter Twelve

Made Rich In Christ

After Jesus uttered the destiny-defining words; 'IT IS FINISHED', the destiny of mankind changed forever. Those words signaled the reversal of contrary conditions and circumstances that had plagued man since the fall of Adam. Poverty, sickness and unfruitfulness to name a few, came to an end because the reason for their continued existence was nullified by Jesus.

Poverty in all its forms was nailed to the cross and buried with Jesus. Jesus bore 'poverty' in His body and was buried with it. When He rose up, He rose up wealthy without poverty. Because you rose with Him, you rose up wealthy and without poverty also.

2 Corinthians 8:9

For we know the Grace of our Lord Jesus Christ

That though He was rich, yet for our sakes He became poor

That you through His poverty might become rich.

Jesus became poor in death so you could become rich in your life. You have been made rich in Christ Jesus. You no longer have to suffer from lack and financial insufficiency. Jesus has made you rich!!

How would you react if one of the richest people in the world informed you they had made you the heir to their fortune? I imagine that news would generate a lot of happiness and excitement in your family and possibly in the country you come from. I want you to understand that something greater than that has happened to you. Somebody richer than the richest man on earth has given you access to His wealth with a blank cheque.

To be precise He has given you a bunch of chequebooks with which you can withdraw from His account what you need at any time. I am talking about the One who created wealth. The One, whose immeasurable wealth can't be compared to that of a mere mortal. Christ Jesus is His name. And it is He who has made you rich. Jesus has granted you access to His inestimable and inexhaustible wealth. HALLELUJAH!!

The physical amount of His wealth that you are able to enjoy depends on you. You determine by faith how much of His wealth to make yours. There has been talk in the Body of Christ for some time about a wealth transfer from the 'world' to saints in the light (believers). I believe this is true.

I also believe the wealth transfer is part of God's divine plan to showcase the glory of His Kingdom. So don't be swayed by news of global economic downturns. The constant drumbeat of doom is all a set up for what God is about to do. The 'light' of your divine wealth will manifest and shine brightest in the darkness of severe global economic conditions.

Light shines brightest in darkness. Light can't shine through where light already exists. Keep focused on the rich promises of God in Christ Jesus and the light of your wealth will soon burst forth.

The children of God are set up to prosper irrespective of dire economic conditions in the world. Your prosperity is not a function of the world economy. Your prosperity is a function of the 'Heavenly economy', which is driven and resourced by God. It does not depend on the economic indicators people appear to 'worship' on earth.

You may be in this poverty-ridden world, but you are not a partaker of it. The children of God are a blessed people who have been called out of poverty to showcase the wealth of God. You have been made rich in Christ and not through the economic means the world teaches and offers.

Charged To The Masters' Card

Without redemption an individual remains under the dominion of sin and by extension under the dominion of poverty. Once redeemed however, you no longer remain indebted to the spirit of poverty. Your indebtedness to the 'overseer of poverty', the devil has been paid off.

1 Corinthians 6:20

For you were bought at a price

Therefore glorify God in your body

And in your spirit, which are God's

This process of redemption can be likened to the purchase of an item with a credit card. During redemption your indebtedness of sin was charged to the Masters' (Jesus') account or better still to the Masters' credit card. Jesus is the Saviour and Master of all mankind. It's to the account of the Master that our indebtedness was credited.

Following man's redemption, all sins, burdens, troubles and financial insufficiency issues have been charged to the Masters' Card. The Masters' Card unlike those given by men is without limit and applicable for past and future debts. It pays for your past, present as well as future indebtedness.

In order for you to be made rich in Christ your sinful debts and liabilities had to be settled and paid off. Not only were your 'sinful' debts paid off, the consequences of your sins including poverty were also paid off. Jesus effected payment on your behalf. He made poverty extinct through the shedding of His precious blood. Every believer has been issued with a 'Masters' credit card'. That is why you should not hesitate to cast your burdens on Jesus. Charge your burdens to the Masters' card.

Everything charged to the Masters' card is paid off by the Blood of Jesus. As you walk in the light of God's Word, you are cleansed of all unrighteousness by the Blood of Jesus. So the blood of Jesus Christ cleanses you of poverty as well as sin. Praise God.

1 John 1:7

But if we walk in the light as He is in the light
We have fellowship with one another
And the Blood of Jesus Christ His Son
Cleanses us from all sin

It's imperative you understand that not only are your 'sinful debts' charged to the Masters' card, your financial debts are charged to it as well. Your finances have been taken care of by Jesus Christ. God says He shall supply all your needs according to His riches in Christ Jesus.

Philippians 4:19

And my God shall supply all your need
According to His riches in glory by Christ Jesus

Your financial needs are not met according to your resources. If you are in Christ, your financial needs are met according to the riches of Christ. Nothing should be financially impossible to you. Therefore refrain from buying into the deception of linking your ability to meet a need to your resources. Charge it to the Masters' card.

Allow your mind to see and prosper in the knowledge that nothing is financially impossible to you in Christ Jesus. Believe and learn to accept by faith that you have been made rich in Christ Jesus. No child of God should flounder in financial debt. No child of God ought to be hiding or running away from creditors.

Declare according to the Word that your debts have been charged to the Masters' credit card. The Master has taken care of all your debts. Acknowledge and meditate on this truth and see it come to pass in your life. Hallelujah!!

Wealth With Purpose

The child of God is not blessed just for the sake of it. You are blessed with a purpose in mind. God is a good administrator of His resources and has a plan for the wealth He places at the disposal of His people. Nobody ultimately owns the wealth that comes into their possession. Men with means are stewards of God's wealth and resources. That's why nobody takes any wealth away with them when they die.

All wealth belongs to our Heavenly Father. He distributes His wealth where it will do the most good and benefit His children. The wealth made available to you as a child of God, is given so others may be blessed by it. You have been put in charge of what does not belong to you. God has assigned you as a distributor of His wealth. You are a channel of God's resources and not the owner of it.

Don't glorify yourself with riches that don't belong to you. By blessing and making you rich God has decided to entrust you with His riches. You have been appointed as a steward to tend and keep His wealth and riches. This is a responsibility not to be taken lightly.

When God blesses you financially, endeavour to be a good distributor of the blessing. Diligence in the distribution of God's blessing facilitates the addition and multiplication of wealth. To him who is generous with what he has received, more will be given.

Reduction and division of wealth are the outcomes for people who are irresponsible stewards of God's wealth. When you are blessed to become a distributing channel of God's riches, ensure you are faithful and diligent in that assignment. It's not only a blessing, but a wonderful privilege as well. When you live your life to be a blessing to others, God will first bless you, and then increase your capacity to be a blessing.

Chapter Thirteen
Your Prosperity Is In Your Mandate

There is a purpose that governs your presence here on earth. You are not here by accident or by chance. God is not given to chances and mistakes. You were uniquely created for a unique purpose and assignment. You were created with a problem in mind and a solution to offer. Accordingly, God has equipped you to confront the problem and provide the solution. This is the mindset every child of God ought to possess. You must have the mindset of being created for a purpose and the ability to fulfill that purpose.

Ephesians 2:10

For we are His workmanship

Created in Christ Jesus for good works

Which God prepared beforehand

That we should walk in them

The recognition of your purpose is a necessary step for the actualization of your prosperity mandate. God is the embodiment of purpose. It's in everything He does. Everything God created was created for a purpose. It can't be possible for any creation of God to be useless.

Ignorance of your purpose can have devastating consequences on your financial state of affairs. This truth is borne in the lives of people who have virtually become beggars due to the ignorance of their purpose.

Potentially great men and women of substance, failed to recognize their purpose, and have turned out nothing like what God envisioned for their lives. Some have become drug addicts, prostitutes, and criminals. Others have paid the ultimate price and died prematurely without achieving their God given purpose.

It must be terribly hard on God, as people He has created for exploits lead lives that are totally at variance with their true worth and potential. They made choices that led them away from their God ordained paths.

Divine Mandate

If you're wondering if you have a purpose, I want to assure you there is one provided you by God. You are the outcome of a divine plan and purpose, not the product of an accident. Because you are the product of a plan and purpose, there is a divine mandate overseeing your presence on earth. That divine mandate is the authority backing you to accomplish your assignment on earth.

There is absolutely no doubt everybody is a solution to somebody or to something. God may not force you to fulfill your function, but your life experiences will be better if you do. Misapplication of purpose neutralizes your mandate. Your mandate 'authorizes' the release of resources for your purpose. Your mandate also 'releases' the benefits and blessing that accrue from fulfilling your purpose.

Mandate is specific to purpose. Meaning, if purpose is misapplied, mandate is ineffective. Consider a scenario where scholarships have been provided for students who enroll in Bible School. If a student selected to attend Bible School rather decides to enroll in Law School, that student has failed to satisfy the conditions for the scholarship.

The mandate of the scholarship board is to fund enrolment in Bible School and not Law School. The Board can't prevent you from enrolling in Law School but it will not fund your stay in Law School. The resources available to the scholarship board can't and will not be applied towards anything apart from enrolment in Bible School.

That is the dilemma facing anyone who operates outside of his or her divine purpose. The wealth that has been made available to you by God is governed by a divine mandate. That mandate is directly linked to your purpose. If the purpose is not fulfilled, the mandate is not activated.

There are people living embittered and frustrated lives because they are engaged in 'adventures' not assigned them by God. Because they have not been assigned to undertake these 'adventures' they are not resourced to fulfil them.

If you live your life outside your purpose, the divine mandate covering your life will not be actualized. When the mandate 'overseeing' your life is frozen in place as it were, life is bound to become a frustrating experience. And when frustration rears its ugly head in your life any measure of success or fulfillment will be hard to achieve.

Activating Mandate

Discovering your purpose is the key to unlocking your mandate. It means getting to know what and who you are. You must be able to identify your abilities and limitations as well as the resources made available to you by grace.

Because you have been designed by God for a purpose you will find tell tale signs of it in your natural life. You will find there are things you do quite easily and very well. Those things come to you naturally almost without any effort on your part. Not only do you do them effortlessly, you enjoy and are fulfilled doing them.

You can also confirm your purpose through prayer and the assistance of the Holy Spirit. Remember the Holy Spirit is supposed to be your comforter and guide. He is also the Spirit of Truth assigned to you to lead you into all truth. Once you discover your purpose, a lifetime of fulfillment is almost certainly guaranteed. You will enjoy your life and be fulfilled by what you do. You will also add value to yourself in doing what you do.

In the pursuit of your purpose, you will find that you will do what you do better than most people. And as you continue in it you will experience the fulfillment of the divine mandate overseeing your purpose. The divine mandate is what will cause doors and opportunities to open before you.

Your provision of a solution to somebody and to something adds value to you. Once you begin to add value to yourself, prosperity will not be far behind. The more value you have, the more people need what you have to offer. Ultimately, the blessing of prosperity you receive from God finds expression through the mandate and the grace on your life.

Diligence

Discovering your purpose alone is not enough. Purpose is only effective and profitable when coupled with diligence. Once you discover your purpose, the diligent prosecution of purpose is what will promote you. The lack of diligence in the pursuit of purpose will inhibit the realization of your full potential.

Success is a child of the diligent prosecution of purpose. With diligence, you will not only enjoy success, you will have good success. A show of diligence by anyone for a purpose was certainly that exhibited by Apostle Paul during his ministry after receiving Christ.

Whenever I picture Apostle Paul going about his business, two words come to mind, diligence and zeal. He couldn't have achieved all he did, as well as writing two thirds of the New Testament without diligence. He knew his purpose, but that alone would not have been enough without the application of diligence. Today we are beneficiaries of his diligence in ministry.

2 Timothy 4:7

I have fought the good fight, I have finished the race, I have kept the faith

This diligence exhibited by Apostle Paul ought to be the standard in the pursuance of our God-given purposes. Diligence begets good success and good success invariably births wealth. It's also in the diligent pursuit of purpose that fortunes are born and made.

Chapter Fourteen

Ambassadors of Christ

You are a citizen of Heaven sent as an ambassador to this world. That means though you are in the world, you are not 'from' the world. So whichever nation in which you happen to find yourself is merely your 'diplomatic post'. That could be the country of your birth or the adopted country in which you live. Whichever the case is, you are there as an Ambassador of Christ to help reconcile people to God and showcase His glory.

2 Corinthians 5:20

Now then, we are ambassadors for Christ

As though God were pleading through us

We implore you on Christ's behalf, be reconciled to God.

Are You Living Like An Ambassador?

The position of ambassador of a nation is an esteemed one and anyone appointed to that office enjoys a great deal of respect. It's a well known fact that the more prestigious a position is, the more attractive the benefits that accompany it. So one can safely assume that ambassadors are well resourced and looked after.

In view of who and what they represent, ambassadors are not the poorest people wherever they are posted to. It will be an oxymoron to claim anyone is as 'poor as an ambassador'. Even ambassadors from the poorest nations on earth can't be described as poor. So how on earth can the Ambassadors of Christ be poor when the ambassadors of men are not?

Based on the revelation of your position as an Ambassador of Christ you ought to ask yourself if you are living like an ambassador where you are. Does your lifestyle match that of an Ambassador from the Kingdom of Heaven?

Ambassadors do not drive deadbeat cars or live in poor and unkempt residential areas. On the contrary they drive in the best cars and live in the nicest neighbourhoods in the countries they are posted to.

I suspect the anti-prosperity folks won't like this much. But unfortunately for them this is the truth and there is nothing much they can do about it. They should remember the streets of Heaven where Ambassadors of Christ come from are paved with GOLD. It's hard to imagine an ambassador from a country where the streets are paved with gold being poor. It's inconceivable.

The ambassadorial status comes with certain perks and privileges, whether you appreciate them or not. You can't pitch a tent in a field as an ambassador and call it your ambassadorial residence, just because you detest prosperity. It's a similar situation to that of being a slave of prosperity. You don't have much of a choice in the matter.

Ambassadors don't live in poverty or struggle to make ends meet no matter where they are posted. At least ambassadors from well-resourced countries or kingdoms such as Heaven don't. They represent the Head of State of their home country wherever they are sent on diplomatic assignments. Thus the ambassadors are well resourced to appear as respectable and distinguished as the position demands.

They have a bearing that suggests an awareness of who and what they represent. They are treated like royalty and as a special class of people. They receive special courtesies and privileges because of their designation as representatives of their countries. They dress well, speak well and carry themselves with grace.

An ambassador from a well-resourced nation like the Kingdom of Heaven shouldn't have to worry about logistics or finances. They should be confident their needs will be met no matter where they are posted to in the world. They don't need to depend on the resources available in the host countries (duty post) to which they have been sent.

Their supply flows from the home country from which they were sent. For the believer your supply flows from the Kingdom of Heaven. Christ, to whom you are anchored is the embodiment of the Kingdom of Heaven and by extension of God.

As an Ambassador of Christ you have been well resourced and programmed not to lack anything. The resources made available to you by your kingdom (Heaven) come as a package with your diplomatic assignment.

There are benefits and privileges that accrue to you because of your designation as an ambassador. Your residence or where you live must be 'ambassadorial' in stature. So must the car you drive and the way you dress. Once you are accredited as an ambassador, your life ceases to be ordinary. Everything about you must reflect who you represent.

The Head of the kingdom you represent as an ambassador is rich and powerful, so your 'ambassadorial projection' to the world must reflect in your dressing, finances and the kind of home you live in. They must all attest to the truth that you an Ambassador from the Kingdom of Heaven.

Begin today to evaluate your circumstances and determine whether they match up to the standard of an ambassador of Christ. If they don't match up, make them match up. You have the power in the Word of God to effect the necessary changes. The Word of God says you are an Ambassador of Christ and your circumstances must reflect this reality.

'Religion' will claim you are an ambassador only in holiness and righteousness. An Ambassador of Christ is unquestionably one in holiness and righteousness, but in wealth as well. Remember you are not only supposed to be as holy and righteous as Christ is. You are supposed to be as rich He is in equal measure. 'As Christ is -holy, righteous and RICH, so are you in this world. Praise God!

As Well Fed As A Church Mouse

I'm hopeful in the not too distant future a new expression - 'as well fed as a church mouse' will be introduced into our everyday speech. This will replace the ignorant expression - 'as poor as a church mouse' that has been used to disparage the Church. I believe this expression, though based on ignorance, is an insult both to God and to the Body of Christ.

But very soon when the Saints of God recognize and assume their rightful position as joints heirs with Christ Jesus, poverty will cease to be synonymous with the Church. The word poverty will no longer be used when talking about the children of the Most High God who is mighty in all things.

God Wants You To Prosper

It's the will of God for you to prosper. Therefore the desire to prosper isn't one based on carnality. It's merely an aspiration to fulfill the will of God for your life. God is disappointed with anyone who fails to appreciate and acquire what He's gone to great lengths to make freely available.

The resources for providing and maintaining your ambassadorial status has been made available by God according to His inexhaustible riches. Never spend a moment, wondering how your transformation from 'rags to riches' is going to manifest. It won't be accomplished with your insignificant resources.

No ambassador is personally responsible for financing the perks and privileges that come with the position. It's taken care of by his or her government. In similar fashion your perks and privileges as an Ambassador of Christ have been provided by the Kingdom of Heaven.

Your financial source is not of this world. You must understand this truth. Your source CANNOT be and is not of this world because you are not of this world. Therefore, don't look to the world or any man as being the key to your well-being. You have already been taken care of by God.

Rise up and live your life as the ambassador of Christ God has made you. God has blessed you with all the possible blessings you'll ever require during your time on earth. Your ambassadorial privileges have been packaged in Christ. As you focus on building your life around Christ they become increasingly available to you.

Ephesians 1:3

Blessed be the God and Father of our Lord Jesus Christ
Who has blessed us with every spiritual blessing
In the heavenly places in Christ Jesus

If Christ abides in you then the blessings are also present in you. The spiritual blessings in Christ are quite different from those available to you on 'retiring' to heaven. Don't confuse the two. There are things meant for you to experience on earth and those you enjoy as part of your 'retirement package' in heaven.

I make this point because 'religion' has brainwashed people into thinking there is nothing but hardship and suffering to be experienced on earth. Religion encourages people to endure hardship even after Christ was almost stripped naked and nailed to a cross in His successful mission to end poverty.

I feed sad when I see people walking around barefooted in medieval robes under the hot sun as a way of showing their submission to poverty. It must cause more pain for Christ to see that than that caused by the nails that were hammered into His body.

These religious folk 'pursue' poverty because they believe it to be God's prescribed way of life on earth. Wealth in their view is only attainable after death in heaven. So they 'graciously and gloriously' live in poverty awaiting death and the blessing reserved for them in heaven.

Obviously the wealth and comforts of Heaven can't be compared to what pertains on earth. After all the logistics of a diplomatic post can't be compared to what exists in the ambassador's country of origin. But that does not also mean the ambassadorial post should be devoid of comfort. The point is that God has made provision for your comfort both on earth and in heaven. God is rich enough and more than capable of blessing you on earth and in heaven. God's will isn't for you to be comfortable only in heaven.

Do Not Fear Lack

An Ambassador of Christ shouldn't live in the fear of lack. Don't be anxious for anything. If the fear of lack begins to well up in your mind, fight it with the Word of God.

One lesson all believers must learn is that you can attract what you fear into your life. If you live in the fear of poverty, you may attract it. Confront any fear with the Word of God to overcome it. Don't try to accommodate and manage it. Fear is like cancer; it spreads and causes real damage if left to fester and not dealt with.

You can invite financial hardship into your life through your fear of lack. Fear is a spirit and has the ability to transport into your life what you live in fear of. Faith is of God, but fear is of the devil. Just as you appropriate the blessings of God by faith, you can appropriate the 'gifts' (curses) of the devil through fear. I describe the devil's 'gifts' as curses because the devil can't bless. Whatever one obtains from him becomes a curse eventually.

When you exercise fear, you cede your authority to the devil and acknowledge his dominion over you. Fear is an open invitation for the devil to manifest himself in your life. But Scripture admonishes believers not to give him any room to operate. This is an important point not to be taken lightly.

Ephesians 4:27

Nor give place to the devil

Without fear the devil can't have access to you. Fear is the devil's access key into people's lives. In the absence of fear the devil can't achieve anything in your life. It's possible your fear of poverty is the reason you are experiencing it right now. 'As a man thinks in his heart so is he'. Be careful what you occupy your mind and heart with.

You are the sum of your thoughts. If you continue to 'meditate' on the financial challenges facing you, they may likely become your reality. What you 'see' and think about the most becomes your reality.

God has not given you the spirit of fear over the lack of money. God has given you power over money and a sound mind over your abundance of money. Poverty is a curse and not a blessing by any stretch of the imagination. Poverty or financial lack is not God's will for you. Stop losing sleep over the fear of poverty. Spend time building yourself up from within by meditating on the blessings God has made available to you.

Chapter Fifteen

Blessed With Every Spiritual Blessing

Financial prosperity is one of the spiritual blessings reserved for you in Christ Jesus. This is an undeniable truth in spite of what those who oppose financial prosperity claim. You have been blessed with every spiritual blessing in Christ Jesus and it includes financial prosperity.

Ephesians 1:3

Blessed be the God and Father of our Lord Jesus Christ

Who has blessed us with every spiritual blessing

In the heavenly places in Christ

The financial portion of your spiritual blessings can be compared to money held in a bank account. You don't see the money, but it is available when you have need of it and make a request for it. Christ represents your bank and all the money you need is available in Him.

Jesus was manifest so that you would have life and have it abundantly (John 10:10). Well that life includes financial prosperity. So in Christ you are destined to have financial prosperity and have it equally abundantly. Financial prosperity is of God and He wants you to have it in abundance without reservation. The children of a rich Father can't be anything else but abundantly prosperous.

The children of God are blessed and prosperous. That is, their status by default and there is no reason to be apologetic or embarrassed about it. After all, it's through no fault of theirs that their Heavenly Father owns all the wealth in the world. You can't help it if your father happens to be rich can you?

It's quite absurd that children of some men are 'expected' to be rich and recognized as such because their parents are rich. But the same is not said about the children of God.

Children of high earning individuals such as professional athletes and business moguls are called rich kids because their parents are rich. But when you are a child of God, the 'world' believes financial insufficiency ought to be your destiny. Isn't that the funniest joke you've ever heard? For me it tops the list of the funniest jokes of all time.

One of the purposes of this book is to help believers define themselves solely by what the Word of God says about them. The Word of God is your standard and not the ill-informed perceptions of the world. If the Word of God says you have been made rich in Christ that settles it.

Your Blessings Already Exist

For many believers grappling with financial lack, their constant prayer is for God to come to their rescue financially. They pray as though they were poor people yet to be blessed by God. When they pray, they literally cry and beg for financial deliverance. I know this firsthand. I also know from firsthand experience, that this kind of prayer is obsolete and not likely to gain any mileage. Why is this kind of prayer obsolete? It's because what your prayer seeks to achieve has already been accomplished.

Well, just imagine a woman constantly praying to God to be made a woman. That's an obsolete prayer if you're already a woman. There is nothing more to be done in that regard. God can do nothing apart from waiting patiently for the day you discover you've been created a woman after all.

Just as a woman can't pray to be made a woman, a child of God can also not pray and beg to be made rich. The 'prayer of begging' is needless to say the least. Christ Jesus has already accomplished what that individual is begging God to do. It happened over two thousand years ago. Instead of begging, the individual should be acknowledging the blessing of wealth and appropriating it. You should not be praying to God to be made rich as though you were a poor person. You've already been blessed financially in Christ.

So why are some people living poor when they are rich in reality? It's because of a lack of revelation. They are rich in reality, but know nothing about that reality. Being rich and living poor is like having money in the bank and not knowing anything about what you have.

That's the conundrum facing many in the Body of Christ. They are rich beyond measure, but have no revelation of it, so they struggle daily in financial insufficiency. But it's not as if God doesn't want to help. He does and has already done so. God wants you rich more than you can ever desire to be because a poor child brings no glory to a rich parent.

Believers need to know the truth about their great financial status in Christ and stop living as 'Rich Poor People'. Their money has been deposited in the bank called Christ Jesus. Money in a bank doesn't come to you. You need to go to the bank to access it. Stop crying and get hold of the Word that will help you 'withdraw' the money.

The Word Is A Transformer

Some believers do have information on their wealth in Christ Jesus, but information alone is not enough. In addition to the information you need revelation of your financial status. It is the revelation that will transform you from a 'rich poor person' into the real rich person God has predestined you to be.

Revelation translates to 'seeing' what the Word has declared. You will not possess your wealth until you 'see' it. You need to see your wealth for your financial metamorphosis to take place. If you can see it, you will have it. Your wealth is a spiritual reality in the realm of the spirit. Because it's a spiritual reality it can only be seen with the 'eye of the spirit' through the Word of God.

I like to describe the Word of God as a 'container of power' with the ability to transform. The Word of God is God in action.

The Word of God is a mirror. When you look in it you will see the image of who and what you are in Christ Jesus. If you continue to behold the image you see in the Word, you will be transformed into what you see. If you see wealth and riches in it, wealth and riches will become your reality. Whatever you find or discover will become your living and experienceable reality.

The power that raised Jesus from the dead is the same power that will transform your financial circumstances. There are people who believe the Word of God for healing but incredibly can't believe the Word to get out of poverty. The Word of God has the power to transform and affect every area of your life.

You have been blessed with 'every spiritual blessing. The blessing of God isn't limited to a specific area of your life. It applies to every area of your life. Once you receive the understanding of spiritual blessings, they will manifest in all areas of your life.

Poverty Mentality

If you possess a poverty mentality, the first option you exercise when you have a financial need is to seek help from man. Immediately thoughts of a need rise up in your mind, you instinctively reach out to friends or family. For people who possess a poverty mentality, their list of financial rescuers doesn't include God. They appear to forget all things are theirs through Christ Jesus and tend to depend on people they can see with their physical eyes.

I used to do that as a 'rich poor person' because I didn't realize God was my only dependable source of help. But when you obtain revelation regarding your provision from God, you will cease to live at the mercy of any man. You come to realize God is your only trustworthy source.

Out of desperation and ignorance, people have put their destinies in the hands of men. They rely on rich friends, spouses and family members, to help them out of their financial challenges. They do so forgetting the people in whom they have reposed their trust are human.

Human beings can only help you when circumstances are within their limited human control. But if you place your trust and confidence in God, you will not lose out. God has ALL circumstances firmly within His control. God may use a man as a channel of blessing, but that man is not the source of your blessing. God remains the source of the blessing and not the man through whom your blessing was delivered.

You are a joint heir with Christ Jesus to all that belongs to God. So by extension all things belong to you. No reliance on any man is required or necessary to meet your financial needs.

1 Corinthians 3:21

Therefore let no one glory in men for all things are yours

Wealth Is Stored In The Word Of God

Your wealth is 'stored' in the Word. You establish what God has declared about your finances with your affirmation and confession of His Word regarding wealth. Anything you will ever need has been packaged into the Word of God. Your wealth is wrapped up in the Word. When you find the Word you will find your wealth.

Acts 20:32

And now, brethren, I commend you to God

And to the Word of His grace

Which is able to build you up and give you an inheritance

Among all those who are sanctified

The Word of God has been designed to build you up in every area of your life. Stick with the Word and it will lead you to your financial inheritance in Christ Jesus.

Chapter Sixteen
You Are Master Of Your Destiny

In the preceding chapters of this book I have written extensively about what God has done to bless His children. I have also written on the role of the devil in the financial hardships of the children of God. In this chapter I would like to dwell on missteps by believers that adversely affect their finances.

Do believers contribute in any way to the circumstances that lead to becoming a 'rich poor person'? I believe the answer is an emphatic yes. Personal responsibility will always play a role in the quality of life of an individual, good or bad.

It's true God has done more than enough to bless you. It's also true the devil is trying his best to steal the blessing from you. The question is what are you doing to receive and retain God's blessing?

The Law of Cause And Effect

I'm a firm believer in the principle of sowing and reaping. This principle postulates that a man shall reap what he sows. This is actually a biblical principle, so it's true whether you agree with it or not. But you must concede to the fact that what you cause to happen always has an effect.

There are believers living as rich poor people because of the choices they have made in their lives. The choices represent the 'cause' and the repercussions are the effects of the cause. The poor quality of their lives has a cause and can't be based solely on what the devil has done to them.

The devil has become a crutch for people who fail to take personal responsibility for their lives. They make poor choices, fail to do what is required, and then blame their misfortune on the devil. Life is full of choices and your life could be the story of the choices you have made so far.

The choices you make in life have an inevitable end. One of my spiritual mentors describes this phenomenon as the 'Law of Inevitable Eventuality'. According to the Law of Inevitable Eventuality, whatever you do produces an inevitable future. Even the failure to make a choice and do something is itself a decision that has an inevitable eventuality. What this means is that you are the architect and master of your own destiny.

It's erroneous to think poverty just happens, like an event; it doesn't. Poverty is a process that takes years to mature based on the choices one makes. In some unique instances however poverty is inherited and not down to choices people make. For people born to poor parents or into poor circumstances the poverty they experience isn't the inevitable result of choices they made. But having said that, being born into poverty doesn't qualify you to remain poor.

Evidence abounds of people born into poverty who managed to turn their lives around at some point in their lives. The dismal financial situation of your parents or guardians can't be wholly responsible for your poor financial situation as a mature adult. Not when you're a child of God.

No matter the kind of start you got in life, it isn't impossible to get back on track. Failing to act or do anything to change the situation is essentially a choice you have made. Any action you take or the failure to take one is a seed you have sown. This seed will produce an inevitable result and future for you.

Just take a look at some of the people you know struggling with financial insufficiency. Some of these people had great opportunities to make their lives better, but failed to do so. They made poor choices and have paid a heavy price for those poor choices.

Seed Time & Harvest Time

There is a principle God has instituted on earth called 'Seed time and harvest time'. This principle applies to everybody on God's green earth. By this principle every human being born of a woman will have an opportunity to earn a living. Everybody is given an opportunity to create and generate income. I repeat everybody. It's God's 'welfare system' for mankind.

Everybody is blessed with opportunities to earn a living by making use of their God-given abilities. God is a wise and complete God. Everybody came into this world programmed with a means to make a living. It's embedded in your purpose and it's your responsibility to recognize and nurture it.

Seed time represent divine opportunities God makes available for people to earn a living. Opportunities don't always translate to receiving creative ideas or starting a business. It could be in the form of employment opportunities because not everyone can start and run a business.

The question is do you sow at seedtime? Or you fail to recognize your seedtime? 'Seed times' are windows of opportunity God creates and we encounter them throughout our lives. Some come big in size. Others are small but lead to bigger and greater opportunities.

The 'action' of failing to sow at seedtime has an inevitable eventuality associated with it. The inevitable eventuality is that there will be no harvest for you to live on because no seed was sown. This could also be described as a harvest of nothing. 'You reap what you sow'. Consequently you will reap 'nothing' if you sow 'nothing'.

That is the essence of the law of cause and effect. Taking the opportunity to sow a seed also has an inevitable eventuality associated with it. The inevitable eventuality is that you will reap a harvest. What you sow is what you reap. If you sow rice you will harvest rice. If you sow a seed of poverty, you will reap poverty.

Seeds of Poverty

Seeds of poverty are actions that over time mature into an inevitable harvest of poverty. I would like to touch on a few I find relevant to believers.

1. **Lack of Bible Study:** People are unknowingly sowing poverty into their lives through the lack of Bible study. The Bible is your life manual and provides divine guidance on how to lead your life. The Word also acts as supernatural seed provided by God to generate everything one needs including money.

   Without the guidance of the Word, you will struggle to recognize opportunities - which seed to sow and when to sow it. Not knowing when to sow means you will fail to reap God's blessings for your life. You can't reap what you have not sown.

2. **Failure to Honour God:** Failure to honour God with your substance and increase is not pleasing to God. It's not a good seed to sow. When you honour God with the little you have, He will respond with His abundance. God loves to honour with abundance, those who are faithful with little.

   Faithfulness with little is a reflection on the nature of your heart. Being unfaithful with little also says a lot about the state of your heart. When you are faithful with little it has an inevitable eventuality. And when you are unfaithful with little, that also has an inevitable eventuality.

   Your faithfulness is an indication of your trust in God and in His ability to meet your needs. The inevitable eventuality of trusting in God is a harvest of abundance. Your unfaithfulness on the other hand, indicates your mistrust in God and His ability to meet your needs. When you fail to trust God you extend a hand in friendship to poverty as an inevitable eventuality.

3. **Tithing:** Failure to give tithe is also one of the surest ways to deny yourself of God's harvest of blessings. It's sad that many don't appreciate the significance of giving tithes to God. I find it incredible that people invest their money with men, yet are unwilling to invest with God. When you give your tithe you are investing in God. Tithing also facilitates the preservation and increase of your blessing. Failure to

tithe opens you up to unplanned expenditures that dissipate your finances.

4. **Procrastination:** This is a seed people sow into their lives as a result of fear. Due to fear people postpone actions the whole world knows they ought to take. Business ideas and concepts have failed to materialize because people failed to act at 'seed time'. They sat on their hands, failed to act and lost potential fortunes. They allowed others to act on 'their' ideas and lost fortunes as a result. Money results from an idea acted upon, not waited upon.

5. **Indiscipline:** Everybody has been blessed with a measure of grace and purpose. The purpose is inherent with provision for meeting the needs of the individual. However, it takes discipline to nurture and abound in your purpose. History is replete with people who flattered to deceive. They failed to live up to their great potential because of a lack of self-discipline.

In the end they relied on the generosity of friends and family members to survive. You may even know former schoolmates who fall into this category. Some of these people are either homeless or begging on the streets. This is the outcome of their failure to discipline themselves and submit to the rigours of academic life.

When others were up early and staying late in pursuance of academic excellence, they chose to sleep or miss class. There are star athletes, politicians and ministers of God who have failed to reach the peak of their calling. They missed out because they could not muster the discipline needed. Their actions and inactions produced an inevitable eventuality of failure.

The Rich Poor Syndrome

The parable of the Prodigal Son in the Bible is one of my favourite parables and one I find quite revealing. There is a significant part of this parable; people don't pay much attention to. That's the part that relates to the elder brother who stayed behind with his father. I like to refer to him as the 'rich poor brother' because his behaviour and actions fall perfectly in line with one suffering from the 'Rich Poor Syndrome.

During a period in my life I didn't know all things were mine in Christ. I didn't realize I was the master of my own destiny. So I kept praying and waiting for God to bless me. But since God had already done all I was asking Him to do, it was a long and disappointing wait. This turned out to be the gestation period of my maturity.

So, though I'm an heir of God's glorious riches, I lived like a 'slave' and in penury. I lived in lack because I was a child in my understanding of God's Word. I was a victim of the Rich Poor Syndrome.

What is the Rich Poor Syndrome? It's a pattern of behaviour exhibited by believers who fail to recognize their access to the blessings available to them. This prevents them from enjoying the blessing of wealth made available by their Heavenly Father.

The 'rich poor brother' should have lived in wealth because his father was extremely wealthy. He was a joint heir to the riches of his father and had access to it. But he didn't have the revelation of his access to the wealth. He didn't enjoy the wealth that had been available to him for years because he didn't know he could.

Just like the 'rich poor son', there are believers who have access to the wealth of their Heavenly Father but lack knowledge of their access. They were made heirs to God the day they gave their lives to Christ. They know they qualify as God's children to enjoy His wealth. Yet they live in misery and in lack. They 'religiously' wait on God for permission they already have through Christ to enjoy His wealth and riches. This pattern of behaviour is the manifestation of the 'rich poor syndrome'.

The Essence of Fellowship

The rich poor syndrome or behaviour exhibited by the 'rich poor son' could be a parable on its own - a parable that teaches about fellowship and grace.

The rich poor son didn't know he was 'permitted' to enjoy his father's wealth because of the lack of fellowship with his father. Fellowship with his father was the key to enjoying the wealth available to him. Unfortunately, he didn't know that.

You are emboldened as a child to enjoy what belongs to your parents when you have a good 'rapport' and fellowship with them. From your own childhood experience you know what a strained relationship with a parent can mean. When fellowship is nonexistent it's pretty difficult to enjoy anything that belongs to your parents.

Your ability to access and enjoy what belongs to your parents is more a function of fellowship than just relationship. The fact that you are related to your parent doesn't automatically guarantee access to what belongs to them. Fellowship and good standing with your parents is what grants you access.

During his self-imposed 'exile', the prodigal son remained a son to his father. The father- son relationship remained intact and was not broken. But he did not have access to the comforts and wealth of his father because of the lack of fellowship.

The elder brother also couldn't enjoy the wealth available to him because of the lack of fellowship with his father. Though he spent all his time in the same house with the father, it made no difference in his life. He had no fellowship with the father. He must have been 'dutiful' but spent no meaningful time with his father.

The situation of the rich poor brother is similar to what a countless number of believers find themselves in. They spend all their time in church 'purportedly' in the presence of God. But they don't have any meaningful fellowship with Him. Some even don't know how to speak to God through prayer.

Their prayers are lengthy and 'meaningless' because they are not based on the Word. They have a 'religious' relationship with God rather than one based on the intimacy of fellowship.

The blessing of our Heavenly Father is made available through fellowship. Lack of fellowship will deny you of the blessing no matter how much time you spend around Him. To fellowship is to spend time with God through His Word, not around Him by merely attending church. The elder brother spent time 'around' his father, but not with his father.

The rich poor son kept himself busy 'around' his father, probably working in the house but didn't spend quality time with the father. You don't enjoy God's blessings by 'performing' to impress Him. You enjoy God's blessing by spending time with Him through fellowship. The 'keys' to accessing the promises of God are given out during fellowship with Him.

This is what the prodigal son did, which the good son did not know to do. The prodigal son returned and 'spent' time with his father. The party to welcome him back home was as a result of quality time spent with his father.

You have been made rich by grace through Christ Jesus and not because you are good or deserving. The prodigal son was restored by grace, and granted access to the wealth of his father through fellowship. He returned home to re-establish fellowship with his father and a party was thrown to welcome him back.

You foster fellowship primarily through the Word. The Word of God is God. The more time you spend in the Word, the more God reveals Himself to you. And as God reveals Himself to you, the inevitable eventuality of that is the manifestation of His glory in your life.

God is excited when you fellowship with Him. He's as excited to get your attention, as you are to get the attention of people who mean something to you. Aren't you more likely to give gifts to people you are intimate with? That's why you give Christmas gifts to members of your family and friends rather than total strangers on the street. Occasionally you may bless strangers but your first instinct is to bless those you share a close relationship or fellowship with. It's no different with God.

The Heir Versus The Slave

As you pursue fellowship with God you mature from childhood to sonship in Christ. Childhood in Christ is a description of one's level of knowledge of the Word. One is described as a child because of the limited knowledge of the Word they possess. An heir of God is described as a child when they lack enough knowledge to appropriate what rightfully belongs to them.

A child in Christ is further described as living like a slave when he or she doesn't enjoy the benefits of the wealth that belongs to them. Therefore you may be a joint heir with Christ to the wealth of God but end up living like a slave because you remain a child due to your limited knowledge.

Galatians 4:1

Now I say that the heir, as long as he is a child

Does not differ at all from a slave, though he is master of all

A child in Christ is immature and childlike in his or her understanding of the Word of God. The immaturity of a believer has nothing to do with physical age. It also has no relation to the number of years one has been 'born again'.

Spiritual maturity is a function of revelation and not experience or duration of church membership. The more you know of the revealed truth, the more mature you become in Christ. Then the more mature you become in Christ, the more the Grace of God abounds towards you. And the more Grace abounds towards you, the more effective your faith becomes. With effective faith, miraculous manifestations of the Glory of God become a common occurrence in your life.

But as long as you remain a 'child', as in your level of knowledge, you will remain like a slave - in bondage to the elements of the 'world', which includes poverty. Thankfully poverty is not a permanent condition. You may have allowed it into your life by remaining a 'child' but you can grow out of it through the knowledge and application of the truth.

To paraphrase one of my spiritual mentors – "You have permitted your present circumstances or they would not exist". What you tolerate, you authorize to exist. Either accept the present situation without complaint or make a decision to use your faith and effect a change'. Grace has been made available to get out of poverty. This grace abounds towards you the more you get to know the 'finished works' of Christ.

2 Peter 1:2

Grace and peace be multiplied to you

In the knowledge of God and of Jesus our Lord

Grace and spiritual maturity are linked to one another. Your level of grace is directly proportional to your level of maturity. In the same manner your level of maturity is directly proportional to the measure of your knowledge of God and of Jesus our Lord. So for the heir (the believer) to claim ownership of what belongs to him, he must mature from childhood to sonship in Christ. It's not acceptable for a believer to experience financial insufficiency or flounder in poverty.

Poverty was nailed to the cross when Jesus was hung on it. Don't tolerate poverty in your life and make the sacrifice of Jesus count for nothing!

Chapter Seventeen

The Key To Prosperity

A major key to unlocking the treasures of heaven is humility. Humility is not only a key, but also a prerequisite to receiving God's blessings. God places a high premium on humility because He who created everything in existence is Himself humble. Your humility is recognition of the Creator's greatness and your commonness. Created from the dust of the earth and without sufficiency in anything, you've been made sufficient in all things in Christ. It's important to God that you acknowledge this by walking in humility.

Philippians 2:5-11

Let this mind be in you which was also in Christ Jesus, Who

Being in the form of God, did not consider it robbery to be equal with God

But made Himself of no reputation

Taking the form of a servant and coming in the likeness of men

And being found in the appearance as a man

He humbled Himself and became obedient to the point of death

Even the death of the cross

Therefore God also has highly exalted Him

And given Him the name which is above every name

That at the name of Jesus every knee should bow,

Of those in heaven and of those on earth and of those under the earth

And that every tongue should confess that Jesus Christ is Lord

To the glory of God the Father

This scripture clearly depicts that the key to God's immeasurable blessings is humility.

Be Humble Like Jesus

The secret behind the success and effectiveness of Jesus was His humility. This character trait is what caused Him to prosper in His mission on earth. Therefore if you desire to be prosperous in all things including your finances, humility must be your central character trait. Humility will help you get ahead in life like wisdom will.

There is promotion in humility. Humility opens great and mighty doors. Humility will bring you closer to God, open doors of opportunity for you, make you friends and confuse your enemies.

Include Some Humble Pie In Your Diet

If you have to constantly remind others of how humble you are, then you are probably not that humble. Genuine humility is practiced not announced so you may need to include a little humble pie in your 'character diet'.

During His time on earth, Jesus humbled himself to the point of submitting Himself to death on the cross. Death by crucifixion represented a humiliating way to die because it was punishment reserved for the vilest of criminals at the time.

But even before being nailed to the cross Jesus was stripped almost naked in preparation for His crucifixion. I can't imagine anyone being happy about being stripped naked and hang publicly for all to gawk at. But the Lord Jesus descended from glory to bring Himself down to such a humiliating level to save you and I. Glory to God!!

He submitted Himself to this humiliation so you wouldn't be poor another day in your life. So before you nonchalantly submit to the evil of poverty be mindful of the sacrifice that ensured that wouldn't happen. Jesus went to great lengths to secure your prosperity. Acknowledge and embrace it.

The sacrifice of Jesus is the most profound act of humility ever recorded and will remain so forever. Thereafter God highly exalted Him and gave Him the name that is above every other name. That at the mention of His name every knee must bow. What does this show? It shows there is a reward in true humility. Hallelujah!!!

Humility Facilitates Grace

Living in humility is not an exercise in futility, because it 'invokes' divine recognition and assistance. Your humility is pleasing to God. It tells Him you acknowledge you have no value without Him. The lack of humility on the other hand will prevent you from accessing your blessing in Christ.

Humility releases the grace of God on your behalf. No one likes to associate with people who are full of themselves. You're more likely to show kindness to a stranger who is polite and respectful than a person who thinks highly of himself. It's basically the same way with God – 'Blessed are those who are poor in spirit'. Humility signals your total dependence on God. As much as God loves you, He won't force His blessings on you. You have to show your appreciation for it to get them flowing in your direction.

Grace is the enabling empowerment from God and is made available in humility. Without the grace of God no child of God can achieve much. If you desire to live up to your potential in Christ you need grace. And to have grace one must walk in humility.

The Animal Called Pride

There is a misconception in the public domain that pride is the preserve of the rich and well to do. But that's not wholly true. Wealth may amplify pride and arrogance, but pride is prevalent among many who lack wealth. I used to be proud and arrogant at some point during my 'sojourn' in financial darkness. I was poor and proud not rich and proud.

I suffered from an inferiority complex brought on by inadequate finances. Therefore, I felt the need to show people I had more wealth than what met their eye! I believe if there is one thing God can't stand or tolerate more than anything else, it must be pride. This claim is not based on conjecture because God says it Himself in His Word.

Proverbs 16:5

Everyone who is proud in the heart is an abomination to the Lord

Though they join forces, none will go unpunished

God will absolutely refuse to be in partnership with anyone who is proud and arrogant. Pride is the quickest way to self-destruction. There is no way you can have any meaningful fellowship with God when you are all puffed up in pride. The grace God makes available isn't compatible with pride. If pride is present, you can be sure; the grace of God will not hang around.

It may take some time to notice the absence of God's grace when you are in pride mode. Therefore don't get complacent if your life appears to be in good shape with your nose in the air looking down on people. If you persist in pride it will only be a matter of time before your 'correction' takes place.

But when you walk in humility the immeasurable blessing of God will overcome and overtake you. The more humble you are, the more grace abounds towards you. It's your humility that gets God rubbing His hands in excitement as He decides how to bless and promote you.

God Resists The Proud

God resists the proud and your pride may be the reason you are failing to achieve the results you have been hoping for. You've probably never considered yourself proud, but you may be living in pride. You can determine that by objectively examining the motives behind your actions. The actions themselves may not tell you much but your motives will indicate if pride is present in your heart.

Pride is very often the hidden reason behind the failure of many believers submitting to the will of God. God is 'immovable' and doesn't submit to anybody's will but His own. When you fail to follow His purpose for your life, you will meet resistance either directly or indirectly from Him.

The resistance you face in going against the will of God doesn't necessarily amount to a punishment from God. The resistance may arise from the fact that you are 'running in a lane not assigned you' or engaged in something you were not designed for.

Imagine for a moment someone attempting to move around a racetrack in a boat. That's going to be impossible because a boat is not designed to move around a racetrack designed for motor vehicles. The boat will be hindered in what it's trying to achieve because it's built to move on water and not on dry land.

The resistance faced by the boat has nothing to do with the manufacturer of the boat. The manufacturer has done his bit and is not the one hindering the movement of the boat on dry land. The boat is being hindered because it's trying to achieve something it wasn't designed to do. So if God designed you as a boat and you persist in moving on land, what exactly do you think is going to happen? You will fail.

God has blessed you with everything you will ever require in your life. But you can only obtain it in line with the divine arrangement put in place specifically for you. The fact that you have money in the bank doesn't mean you can break in, when you need money. If you try that you will be resisted. You can only withdraw your money from the bank the right way.

Pride can show up in the lives of people when the blessing of God gets to their heads. Such people face the possibility of facing resistance from God at some point in their lives. Pride and resistance go together. Where there is pride there is bound to be resistance along the line. It was pride that got the devil where he is today!!!

Humility is an indication of submission to the will of God whiles pride is synonymous with rebellion against God. I'm sure you don't want to suffer anything close to what the devil will experience for the rest of his miserable existence because of pride.

I urge you to examine your life closely for signs of pride because it can creep into your heart without you being conscious of it. Pride could be the source of your financial stagnation and nothing to do with the devil.

2 Corinthians 3:5

Not that we are sufficient of ourselves

To think of anything as being from ourselves

But our sufficiency is from God

To serve as a check against pride creeping into my heart, I constantly remind myself of who and what I am - which is nobody and nothing without Christ. I endeavour to do this, especially in moments when the demon of self-aggrandizement tries to engage my mind.

In my bible study classes I tell my students, whatever they achieve in their lives as believers has nothing to do with them. Their glorious end is the handiwork of Christ. He gives grace, wisdom; knowledge, understanding and ability to enable us achieve what we have been mandated to do.

Let God Be Your Reputation

One of the secrets to fight pride and ensure success is to make yourself of no reputation, and allow God to be your reputation. God loves to work with the weak and foolish things of this world, that are looked down upon. That's how the glory of the Lord is revealed. When you allow God to be 'large and in charge', it may make you look feeble and foolish by the standards of the world. However, I can assure you it's a small price to pay in exchange for God's awesome glory and power.

The world may consider you 'feeble and foolish' but the 'feeble and foolish' are the kind of people and material God is always looking out for to demonstrate His glory. 'Feeble and foolish' people represent the 'canvas' God requires to paint His masterpieces on.

The Bible is replete with people like David who were looked down upon but rose from being nobody to somebody. That's how God loves to manifest His glory. David was promoted from shepherd boy to the greatest king in the history of the nation Israel and Joseph from prisoner to Prime Minister of the greatest nation at the time. Only God can make this happen. Hallelujah!

Mathew 23:12

Whoever exalts himself shall be abased

And he who humbles himself shall be exalted

It's in your weakness that God demonstrates His strength and it's in your inability that God shows His ability. Don't try to be wise and able. Acknowledge your weakness in humility and allow God to be your wisdom and ability.

2 Corinthians 12:9

And He said to me, 'My grace is sufficient for you

For my strength is made perfect in weakness

Therefore most gladly I will boast in my infirmities

That the power of Christ may rest upon me

2 Chronicles 7:14

If My people who are called by My name will humble themselves

And pray and seek My face and turn from their wicked ways

Then I will hear from heaven and will forgive their sin and heal their land

Chapter Eighteen
Your Wealth Is A Spiritual Reality

God is a Spirit and He lives and operates from the spirit realm. Consequently the spirit realm represents the universe's seat of power because that is where God dwells. That simply means it's from the spirit realm that events on earth are determined. The spirit realm oversees the physical realm, thus what pertains to you in the spirit realm determines your natural circumstances.

The spirit realm is not 'fantasy land' or an imagined location. God is real and exists as a Spirit Being. Therefore spiritual things are real and do exist. If spiritual things are real and exist, then your spiritual blessings in heavenly places are also real and exist. Hallelujah.

The world you live in together with most of the things in it may appear to exist physically, but they are founded on the spiritual. The earth is the realm of manifestation of the things you see and not the source of it. The physical state is merely the state of manifestation.

In other words the physical state is the state in which spiritual things physically express themselves in order for them to be seen and experienced. The physical state is not the original state of the things you see. Pastor Kenneth Hagin of blessed memory describes it this way - 'all things physical first existed in the spirit realm'.

The Word of God and the promises of God exist as spiritual realities. This requires the Believer to live by faith and not by sight because spiritual realities can only be pursued by faith - with the eye of the spirit. If you live to see with your physical eyes before you believe you won't obtain the promise. The believer believes before he sees the promise become reality. Things that are seen physically are the manifestation of spiritual realities.

Spiritual Realities Represent Your True Reality

The promises of God captured in His Word represent spiritual realities - they are real but spiritual in nature. The new man in Christ is a spirit being and a product of the Word of God which is also spiritual in nature. Everything the Word says about the new man in Christ is a spiritual reality. Therefore spiritual realities represent the true reality of a child of God.

Your natural circumstances should reflect your spiritual realities in Christ Jesus. Therefore the state of your finances should reflect the spiritual reality of your abundant wealth in Christ. Any situation that is contrary to this constitutes a mirage. According to the Word of God, Christ has made you rich. Therefore any poverty defining circumstance you encounter is temporary and can't be permanent.

The fact that Christ has made you rich should be settled in your mind. Just because you are yet to experience it doesn't negate the truth that you are exceedingly rich in Him. But like every other blessing you have in Christ, financial sufficiency is a spiritual reality that needs a 'faith transformer' to step it down to your physical level.

Never be in doubt about your wealthy status. If you believe in the existence of Christ and in His finished works then you must believe in your prosperity. This prosperity has nothing to do with you. It's about Christ. You're not rich because you're hardworking but because Jesus Christ to whom you have been joined is rich. And as long as Jesus remains rich so will you.

However the wealthy status of the believer is a spiritual reality and requires transformation into a physical reality before it can be enjoyed on earth. Spiritual realities are the true realities of the new man in Christ. The contrary physical circumstances you see with your optical eyes don't constitute your reality. Physical circumstances are not 'real' because they are temporary - fleeting, transient, short-term, short-lived, brief, passing, interim, momentary and impermanent.

Spiritual realities on the other hand are eternal - everlasting, undying, unending, perpetual, endless, timeless, ceaseless, interminable and forever. They don't expire or go out of fashion because they're founded in Christ. Physical circumstances expire and become obsolete, but spiritual realities do not.

Believers must learn to 'see' what the Word says as opposed to what natural circumstances reveal. Many encounter difficulties experiencing the promises of God because they're challenged in accepting the existence of spiritual realities. Be assured spiritual realities are as real as the God you believe in. People struggle to believe in spiritual realities because they haven't been able to fathom how they exist.

The fact that you can't see bacteria doesn't mean they don't exist. They do but can only be seen through a microscope. In the same vein spiritual realities exist but can only be seen through the eyes of faith. Your wealth is a reality established in the spirit realm. God has established it and it can't be undone or reversed. This is the truth and you must uphold it with conviction.

2 Corinthians 4:18

While we do not look at the things which are seen

But at the things which are not seen

For the things which are seen are temporary

But the things which are not seen are eternal

Poverty Is Transient And Not Real

If physical realities are fleeting and brief, then the existence of financial insufficiency for a believer is fleeting and brief also. It can't last forever. The wealth of a believer on the other hand is a spiritual reality - eternal, unending, endless, interminable, perpetual, never-ending, ceaseless, everlasting and undying. Because your wealth is a spiritual reality its physical manifestation is interminable.

One overlooked cause of financial insufficiency is the attribution of God's blessing to a physical source or man.

God's blessings don't originate from physical sources. It's like expecting fish to walk on land or horses to live on trees. When you ascribe God's blessing to a wrong source, it hinders its flow.

Correctly recognize that spiritual realities of provision come from God and acknowledge Him as the source of it. When you acknowledge God this way, He will establish Himself as Provider in your life.

God can bless you with an idea to sell ants and enable you build a fortune doing that. He can bless you with an idea that may never occur to you in a million years! God can make you rich, whichever way He wants; even through the selling of ants!!

But you inch closer to poverty when you attribute blessings to men rather than God. No man can bless. Men can only facilitate that which God has already ordained. But many look to men then become frustrated and angry with God when their expected blessings fail to materialize.

Location Of Spiritual Realities

The rich promises of God can seem remote and unobtainable because they are located in Christ. Nonetheless, with understanding, you will appreciate that their location is the best thing that could have happened.

Christ represents the most secure location to keep your blessings because it is one place the devil CANNOT reach. The devil is a thief with an agenda to steal from the children of God at the least opportunity. Knowing the nature of our adversary, God must have placed His blessings in Christ to keep them out of reach of the devil.

By placing our blessings in Christ, they are made secure and accessible at the same time. Your wealth has not been hidden away from you by God but secured in Christ. If your wealth is in Christ and Christ dwells in you, then your wealth is directly accessible to you.

Your wealth is not in the hands of anyone apart from you. If Christ dwells in you, your wealth can't be anywhere else but in you. Your blessings couldn't be more available to you than that. Their location also implies you're the only one with access to them. No one else apart from Christ has access to what's in you but you.

If they were kept anywhere else, they would not be as secure and available to you. Your wealth has been in you for as long as Christ has been in you. So you have access to it right now. You don't need anybody's permission to use and enjoy your blessing. It's within reach whenever you need it. Praise God.

Your wealth in Christ is a reality you must understand and appreciate. The reason your wealth has appeared to be remote is because you have failed to recognize it as a spiritual reality already available in you.

You Need A Change Of Mindset

If you need a change in your financial circumstances know that God acting through Christ Jesus has done His part. Now you must do your part to effect the change you seek in your finances. The change must begin with a change in your mindset, based on the truth revealed to you.

Romans 12:2

And do not be conformed to this world

But be transformed by the renewing of your mind

That you may prove

What is that good and acceptable and perfect will of God

The change you seek in your finances must start with a paradigm shift in what you perceive to be real. You must begin to see and accept the realities espoused in the Word of God as your realities. Don't conform to the poverty mentality of the world. In order for you to prosper, your mind must first prosper. You must traverse this step to make any progress.

Renew your mind with the new reality in Christ. Your mind must visualize and accommodate your prosperity. This must happen before the physical manifestation of your prosperity can take place. If you can't see it with your mind, you can't have it in your hand.

Joshua 1:8

This Book of the Law shall not depart from your mouth

But you shall meditate in it day and night

That you may observe to do according to all that is written in it

For then you will make your way prosperous

And then you shall have good success

So how do you get your mind to see your prosperity? By feeding and meditating on scriptures that speak about your prosperity. Meditate on them day and night. Consider nothing else but the Word of God so you can make your way prosperous.

You have been made rich in Christ Jesus and this is the truth you need to feed on without ceasing. Don't waste your time lamenting over the poor state of the economy. You are not of this world and therefore can't be affected by the economic conditions that pertain in it. The economy that governs your circumstances is the economy of Heaven. Praise God.

If you feed on the negative economic news that the world churns out, it will become your reality. What you believe as real eventually becomes your reality. Disregard visible circumstances and dwell on spiritual truths and realities.

Abraham didn't consider his one hundred year old body; when he was promised a child by God. Neither did he consider the state of Sarah's body, which was pretty old too.

When Abraham wanted a child he focused on the spiritual reality he had received and didn't dwell on the challenges visible to him. He couldn't have believed God, if he had given attention to the prevailing circumstances facing him.

Romans 4:19

And not being not weak in faith

He did not consider his own body already dead

(Since he was about a hundred years old)

And the deadness of Sarah's womb

He did not waver at the promise of God through unbelief

But was strengthened in faith giving glory to God

And being fully convinced that what He had promised

He was also able to perform

Your transformation is directly related to your ability to accept the spiritual realities in the Word of God. Nobody can do this for you. Feed on scriptures that speak of God's blessings to His children. Meditate on them till they become conscious realities in your mind.

The change in reality from poor to rich in Christ must be accompanied by a change in the way you speak. Your verbal expressions and choice of vocabulary must reflect the paradigm shift. You must stop using expressions like 'I don't have money or I can't afford it'. You have all the money you need in Christ and can afford anything.

Your God is committed to supplying all your needs according to His inexhaustible riches and budget. Not according to your exhaustible riches and limited budget. Because you're a new creation in Christ Jesus, your purchasing power has ceased to depend on you or what you can afford.

Your purchasing power is based on the riches of God vested in Christ Jesus. This must be your mindset. Be consistent and disciplined in this effort to transform your life. If you are faithful in this exercise, it won't be long before your wealth becomes physically evident in your life. Hallelujah!!

Chapter Nineteen
Bridging The Manifestation Gap

I believe after reading up to this point you are fired up and ready to obtain what rightfully belongs to you. But before you begin to stake your claim you need to know how to negotiate the manifestation gap. The manifestation gap is the period between the time of believing in a spiritual reality and its transformation to physical realities that can be experienced. The gap represents the transition from believing God's word and experiencing what Jesus has accomplished. That is the gap between exercising faith and the manifestation of God's Word.

This space of time can represent a major hurdle to negotiate for many people.

For many years though I 'believed' God's Word, I struggled to experience the manifestation of what I had come to believe. The inability to experience the precious promises of God after people have appeared to believe is a major dilemma. They hear the Word of God, believe it and yet are unable to experience what they have heard and believed.

The How

The first step to bridging the manifestation gap is to be convicted about the truth you have come to know. You must believe it with the conviction and innocence of a child. You must adopt the attitude that if God has said it then it is what He says it is. You must decide to believe what the Word says and disregard all other viewpoints.

After making the decision to believe by faith, progress to accepting what you have come to believe as a spiritual reality that exists even though you can't see it. You can't remain at only believing in healing for example. You must see healing as a spiritual reality. You get to this point through the consistent and diligent meditation on God's Word. Your conviction must be strong on the existence of spiritual realities. If you are not convinced you can't bridge the gap.

During this process spiritual realities must become rhema for you. When you get hold of it as rhema, refuse to let go. Literally hold on to it for dear life. Hold on like Jacob held onto the Angel of the Lord and refused to let go. Don't be swayed by arguments contrary to the rhema that has come into your possession. Your change will manifest in the revelation you have received.

The final step in bridging the faith gap involves the affirmation of the spiritual realities you have come to believe. That is the key to physically experiencing the spiritual realities available to you through Christ Jesus. Your affirmation by faith triggers the transformation of spiritual realities into physical manifestation on your behalf.

Begin to 'see and claim' the realities like Abraham did when he looked up into the night sky after receiving the promise of God. Abraham began to see the children he had prayed for instead of the stars that lit up the sky. He affirmed the stars as his children and descendants by faith.

Philemon 1:6

That the sharing of your faith

May become EFFECTIVE

By the acknowledgement of every good thing

Which is in you in Christ Jesus

The word effective in the scripture above refers to something that is successful in producing an intended or desired result. It also means productive, potent, effectual, powerful, constructive and efficacious. That translates to mean your faith becomes productive, successful, potent, efficient, powerful, constructive and efficacious when you acknowledge the spiritual realities that are in you through Christ Jesus.

Your verbal affirmation of the spiritual realities you believe in sets a spiritual process in motion. This process transforms hitherto spiritual blessings into physical realities that will address your needs and circumstances.

2 Corinthians 9:8

And God is able to make all grace abound toward you

That you, always having all sufficiency in all things

Have an abundance for every good work

Deuteronomy 15:6

For the Lord your God will bless you

Just as He has promised you

You shall lend to many nations, but you shall not borrow

You shall reign over many nations

But they shall not reign over you

Your blessing is within you and awaiting acknowledgement to be birthed into physical manifestation. You must make a habit of consistently acknowledging the spiritual realities that are in you in Christ Jesus. To bridge the manifestation gap you must focus on Jesus, the Author and Finisher of your faith and disregard everything else.

Christ In You The Hope Of Glory

Christ in you is indeed the hope of glory. If spiritual realities are available in Christ and Christ dwells in you, then you are bound to experience glory in all your circumstances. Hallelujah. Christ living in you is an awesome spiritual reality. It's a literal experience and not a figurative one. Christ literally lives in you!!! That's confirmation that you are the Body of Christ, His flesh and His bones. He lives in you with the fullness of His grace; including the grace of wealth (John 1:16).

Ephesians 5:29-30

For no one ever hated his own flesh, but nourishes it and cherishes it

Just as the Lord does the church
For we are members of His body
Of His flesh and of His bones

Galatians 2:20

I have been crucified with Christ it is no longer I who live,
But Christ lives in me
And the life which I now live in the flesh, I live by faith in the Son of God
Who loved me and gave Himself for me

John 1:16

And of His fullness we have all received
And grace for grace

Your blessing of wealth resides in Christ Jesus. Every blessing made available to you by God is available in Christ Jesus. Therefore if Christ is in you, where do you think the blessings are? They are in you. Praise God.

Ephesians 1:3

Blessed be the God and Father of our Lord Jesus Christ
Who has blessed us with every spiritual blessing
In the heavenly places in Christ

Ephesians 3:20

Now to Him who is able to do exceedingly abundantly
Above all that we ask or think, according to the power that works in us.

God is able to do exceedingly and abundantly above all that we ask or think, according to the power that works in us. Hallelujah!! The power to effect change is in you. And how do you engage this power? You engage it by acknowledging the spiritual realities that are in Christ Jesus and in you.

The Manifestation Is Now

The manifestation of spiritual realities is always 'now' and not at a later date. The reason for that is simple – they already exist. But on occasion the devil uses time as a tool to deceive and delay expectations. Therefore believers need to know the promises of God are all in the present and not in the future. God wants you to receive now and not later.

Whatever you need already exists and has been provided. They are not visible to your optical eyes because they exist in the pre-manifestation state. The pre-manifestation state is the condition in which all things exist prior to their physical manifestation.

The efficiency of your faith primarily determines the speed at which your spiritual reality is transformed from the pre-manifestation to an experienceable state. It has little to do with time. It's the devil who tries to get you to put a time frame to your blessing. The more efficient your faith is, the quicker your blessings are released.

When you acknowledge the spiritual realities in you, remember they are in existence now. Your prosperity is right now and not timed to the projected improvement in your country's economy. Don't rationalize or make excuses for your lack of faith by putting a time frame to the manifestation of your blessings. And don't allow anybody to do that for you either.

The more you acknowledge and expect in the now, the more effective your faith will become. Remember your expectation doesn't exist in a vacuum. It's based on tangible realities that exist in Christ. When you exercise faith to appropriate spiritual realities you're not engaged in wishful thinking. They're as real as you are.

Chapter Twenty

The Truth Set Me Free

Once upon a time poverty was the devil's plan for me and I didn't have the knowledge to contest it. Therefore, though I have been made rich in Christ, I endured hardship like a slave. I suffered needlessly because I remained a child in the knowledge of the Word.

Galatians 4:1

Now I say that the heir as long as he is a child

Does not differ at all from a slave

Though he is master of all

In this book I have disclosed my discoveries of the timeless truths of the Gospel of Jesus Christ. This is what helped me break the back of financial insufficiency in my life. The Word literally became a lamp onto my feet and light onto my path.

As I became enlightened, I began to appreciate that financial insufficiency was not my preordained destiny. God's desire is for everyone to prosper but this will happen as people's understanding of His Word 'prospers'.

3 John 1:2

Beloved I pray that you may prosper in all things

And be in health just as your soul prospers

It's the truth, the knowledge of the gospel truth that finally set me free. I discovered that God was not responsible for making me poor, because He created me to be rich. Neither did He require me to endure a wilderness poverty experience. He only wanted me to mature and come into the knowledge of His Word. Once I matured and gained knowledge I was free to enjoy my inheritance as His son.

Discovery Of My Blessing

During the process of my enlightenment one exciting discovery I made was the fact that all blessings available in Heaven had been reserved for me in Christ. I discovered Jesus was not only my Saviour but also my Vault of heavenly treasures.

Ephesians 1:3

Thanks be to God and the Father of our Lord Jesus Christ

Who has blessed us with every blessing in heavenly places in Christ Jesus

'Ephesians 1:3' is one of my 'enlightenment scriptures' because it helped open my eyes to my blessing in Christ. This is the scripture from which I received revelation that EVERY blessing in heaven had been made available to me in Christ Jesus.

All the years I had needlessly endured financial insufficiency as a Christian, was only because of my ignorance. I already had every blessing provided for me in Christ and I knew nothing about it. I had lived for years as a 'rich poor person' rather than the person I was in Christ Jesus due to ignorance.

As the light of revelation began to flood my mind, a lot of scriptures began to open up to me. These scriptures revealed a lot of things about the nature of my provision in Christ to me. Another one of my enlightenment scriptures was Philemon 1:6.

Philemon 1:6

That the sharing of your faith may become effective

By the acknowledgement of every good thing

Which is in you in Christ Jesus

From this scripture I got to understand that the blessings in Christ Jesus become available through the acknowledgment of them. To acknowledge something is to take notice of that thing. That means prior to my enlightenment, my blessing in

Christ hadn't become available because I failed to notice it. I took notice of the financial insufficiency around me but failed to acknowledge the wealth within me in Christ Jesus.

I look back on my years of financial insufficiency and the 'monster' it turned me into. For many years I was withdrawn, moody, agitated, irritable and distressed because of my stressful financial situation. I put on a façade of being happy but deep down I was troubled and unhappy. I was 'perishing' because of my lack of revelation knowledge.

Hosea 4:6

My people are destroyed for lack of knowledge

Because you have rejected knowledge

I also will reject you from being priest for Me

Because you have forgotten the Law of your God

I also will forget your children

But once I knew how to get what was mine, what is mine became mine. Hallelujah. It's my very fervent prayer that as you read the collection of 'timeless truths' recorded in this book, you shall receive this revelation also. Then what you are entitled to, shall surely become yours in Jesus' name.

Allow the Word of God to build you up and transform you from a 'rich poor person' to the real rich person that you really are. May the Grace of our Lord Jesus Christ, immeasurably abound toward you and empower you get your finances on track.

Your wealth is a spiritual spirituality that is established. It can't be reversed or annulled, so go ahead and possess it. You have been made rich in Christ. Christ in you can only mean a life of eternal sufficiency and certainly not poverty. Amen.

END

About The Author

Kwaku Agyeman is a Teacher of the Word of God by grace and calling. He is also a family and life counselor and a graduate of Central University College's School of Theology & Missions. He is the founder and CEO of Entrepreneurship & Technology Center and an independent publisher of Christian, educational and children's eBooks.

He derives great fulfillment from empowering people to achieve their God given potential. He also has a real passion for teaching, motivating and helping build people up through the Word of God. He describes his heart's greatest desire as seeing people overcome poverty and sickness through knowledge of the Word of God.

Discover Other Titles By Kwaku Agyeman

Prosperity Passport

Rise Up & Walk

Healing Medicine

The Search For Grace

Living Under The Influence

Faith Is Not Imagination

Rest In Praise

Spiritual Emphasis

Behold & Become

Recipe For Rest

Acknowledgements

I would like to acknowledge all who helped make this book possible. And I begin by first of all giving thanks to my Heavenly Father, whose work this is in reality. He is the Author of this book and I am merely privileged to physically put it together. I am humbled and deem it an honour working with You on this project.

I would also like to thank my wife Naana for your patience in bearing the inconvenience I put you through in the course of writing this book. When I found you, I really found a good thing and it accounts for the favour I have obtained from the Lord.

Another round of thanks goes to my brother Dr. Yaw Donkoh for his help in publishing this book as well as those who helped me in formatting it.

Finally, I would like to thank my parents, spiritual mentors, siblings, friends, the members and leadership of the International Central Gospel Church, TBN, Daystar and The Word Network who have all helped in making this work possible.

Thank you all & God Bless

Kwaku Agyeman

www.ingramcontent.com/pod-product-compliance
Lightning Source LLC
Chambersburg PA
CBHW070657220526
45466CB00001B/481